Redesigning Your Health

A Road Map to Self-directed Healing

By
Laura Brown

Chattahoochee Chase Publishing
Atlanta, GA

COPYRIGHT

The content of this book is for general instruction only. Each person's physical, emotional, and spiritual condition is unique. The instruction in this book is not intended to replace or interrupt the reader's relationship with a physician or other professional. Please consult your doctor for matters pertaining to your specific health and diet.

To contact the author, visit www.intuitive-wellness.com

Printed in the United States of America

Contents

Introduction: The Color in the Pot   1

Part I ~ The Terrain   6

Chapter 1 ~ The Need for Self-direction   7

1.1 The Days of the GP   8

1.2 Not about Western Medicine Versus Alternative   10

1.3 It Is about a Flexible System   11

1.4 Signs of Change   12

1.5 Issues Resolved with this Approach   13

1.6 Why Move Away from Conventional Healthcare?   14

1.7 My Goal   15

Chapter 2 ~ A Simple Method   17

2.1 Four Dimensions of Healing   17

2.2 Synergistic Healing   20

2.3 Operates as a Road Map   22

2.4 Benefits of My Approach   22

2.5 What is required?   23

2.6 Synergistic Healing Requires a Change of Mindset   24

2.7 Synergistic Healing Requires a Shift to Wellness   26

Chapter 3 ~ Setting Up Conditions for Success   33

3.1 Getting Help (Environment of Support)   34

3.2 How to Work with Health Care Providers and Stay in Control of the Direction   35

3.3 Having a Plan of Your Own   39

3.4 The Best Doctors-Providers Want Their Clients to Do This   41

3.5 It's Not About Opposition or Rebellion Against Any Outside Authority   42

3.6 It Is About Being Your Own Authority - Empowering Yourself   43

3.7 A Little Along   43

Part II ~ Steps of the Method   45

The Simple Method ~ A Seven-Step Process   48

Step 1 ~ Triggering Event   51

Step 2 ~ Decision and Impact of Decision   60

Step 3 ~ Explore & Organize   68

Step 4 ~ Make Choices about Approach, Feelings, Changes   75

Step 5 ~ Monitor and Adjust   83

Step 6 ~ The Turning Point   89

Step 7 ~ A Wellness Adventure   95

Part III ~ Applying the Simple Method   102

Applying the Process   103

Profile 1 ~ Our Patient with Rheumatoid Arthritis   107

The Triptych – How She Navigated Her Journey   108

Profile 2 ~ The Registered Nurse   112

The Triptych – How She Navigated Her Journey   113

Profile 3 ~ The Mom   116

The Triptych – How She Navigated Her Journey   117

Conclusion   120

Appendix and Resources   122

Template for Action Plan   122

Sample Action Plan   125

Acknowledgments   128

About the Author   130

Introduction: The Color in the Pot

Many years ago, I had the good fortune to meet a nun by the name of Sister Annette Covatta, when I was attending a Journal Workshop that she was facilitating based on the work of Ira Progoff. In that workshop, Sister Annette told a story I've never forgotten, called simply "The Color in the Pot." I would like to recount that story here by way of introduction to the intention of this book.

There once was a village in a remote area of a medieval kingdom. Once or twice a year, a dye-master would travel to this remote village, bringing her many colored potions. Early in the morning, she would set up her cauldron at the pavilion in the center of town, building a small fire underneath. There she would ply her trade all the long day, adding wood to the fire periodically.

And every time the dye-master visited, the local citizens would line up with their fabrics and materials to have them dyed. On this one particular day, the first customer stepped up to the cauldron with her bolt of cloth and the dye-master said:

"Welcome fine lady. And what color would you like today?"

"I'll have the azure blue of the sky above" said the lady.

And the dye-master dipped the cloth into the pot with a swirl, and pulled out a fabric dyed a beautiful azure blue just as the woman had requested.

Happy with her fabric, the woman paid the dye-master and took her leave as the next person stepped up.

"What color will you have today?" she asked of the gentleman.

"I'll have the yellow of the daffodil, please" he replied.

Again the cloth was lowered into the pot and retrieved; this time dyed the perfect daffodil yellow.

So the day went, the dye-master producing colors from meadow green, to rose red, all as requested by each of her customers in turn.

Throughout the day, there was one villager, an old man, sitting on a nearby bank watching the day's commerce unfold. And late in the day, as the villagers all had their requests fulfilled and departed for home, he slowly made his way down from the hill, approaching the dye-master by himself, the last customer for the day.

"Welcome esteemed old one" the dye-master spoke. "What color will you have today?"

And with a twinkle in his eye, the old man pointed to the cauldron, saying "there are many beautiful colors you could produce for me, as I've learned by observing you today. But for me, it's not the blue of sky or the green of glen. For myself, I'd like the color in the pot."

The old man didn't want "a" color. He wanted the source of all colors. He wanted the color behind all colors, and the ability to create for himself any color he might wish.

I tell this story to illustrate the intention of this present work, which is to distill a method that anyone can learn to take charge of their own health and healing.

There are many books on the market today that address a particular condition, such as the "I Cured My Arthritis and You Can Too" type book. I enjoy these books and believe they can provide considerable value. And indeed, I have several on my shelf. But they're not the kind of book I wanted to write.

I'm interested in the story behind the books. The story of the healing journeys taken by the people who wrote those books. And the stories of the many people who have taken similar healing journeys without writing a book.

I do believe that among these people who are taking charge of their own health, we're seeing a new model, one that's sourced more in our future than in our past. And I see these modern-day healers of self and others as harbingers of a new world that's coming from our futures into our present day lives.

> *You are always free to change your mind and choose a different future, or a different past.*
> **– RICHARD BACH**

I have had my own healing journeys, where I chose to leave the beaten path of conventional medicine and make my own way. I believe there are similarities between my journey and those other people's which are worth exploring in order to come up with a road map that anyone who wants – or needs – to take charge of their own health could benefit from.

Throughout my thirty-year career as a business technologist, one of my specialties has been business process improvement, the re-engineering of the corporation. And it made sense to me to take the design skills I developed over the years and apply them to do the following three things for personal health:

- **Map** the terrain of self-directed healing.
- **Identify** the steps or stages of the healing journey.
- **Chronicle** what occurs for people at each of those stages in order to provide a road map.

This approach is not about changing the health-care system; it's about changing your own personal system. Part of what's "wrong with this picture" of the current health-care system is that we're so externally focused, looking for the fix from drugs, doctors, or other practitioners.

It's about taking personal responsibility for your own health. When you do learn to take personal responsibility for your own health, everything changes. That's where the power is. It's also about self-reliance.

As I conducted process-improvement projects in corporations, I found that one of the most important aspects for my clients is helping them stay in the driver's seat. The process and the information can be confusing and overwhelming to clients, as it often is in healthcare. It's easy to want to turn to an expert or an authority, and just let them tell you what to do.

In corporate settings, you lose control of the project (and often the budget) if you give in to that temptation. The same is true for our health-care choices. It's easy to think we have to find the "right" authority, whether they be a doctor, author or other practitioner, and follow their instructions. The problem with this approach is that it is dis-empowering.

> *If you believe the doctors, nothing is*
> *wholesome;*
> *if you believe the theologians, nothing is*
> *innocent;*
> *if you believe the military, nothing is safe.*
> — LORD SALISBURY

This book is about my experiences, and those of others, in staying empowered in my health-care choices, and about showing you how you can do the same. It's about the approach and process, not about the content (my individual health issues and treatments), although there's quite a bit of information in the content for specific issues. It's about becoming your own advocate in your health-care choices.

PART I

~

THE TERRAIN

Most people would like to be delivered from temptation but would like it to keep in touch.

— ROBERT ORBEN

Part I discusses the context of health care and healing in America today, the origins of the method and how to create an environment of support for your healing.

This section of the book comes out of my own experience and those of my clients and the women I interviewed for this book.

Chapter 1

~

The Need for Self-direction

*To bring anything into your life, imagine that
it's already there.*

— Richard Bach

The first thing to notice about self-direction is that you're already doing it. You already make choices and decisions about your own health and health care, whether in a completely independent way, or by way of choosing your doctor and following her advice. You're already responsible for your health choices. The question to ask yourself is: How conscious are you of that responsibility?

Do you embrace the responsibility of your health choices, or try not to think about it? Wherever you are along the spectrum between the two poles of embracing versus avoiding, this book is intended to help you move toward the embracing side of the equation.

If you do become more self-directed about your health, you won't be alone. More and more people are quietly taking charge of their health and moving away from standard American healthcare toward an approach characterized by self-direction.

A quiet revolution has people looking beneath the surface, and taking charge of their health. I know because I've done it. I've been practicing self-reliant health for more than

30 years. I know it's possible, and I can show you how to develop a plan that you construct yourself, tailored to your own unique situation and requirements.

My healing journey started back in 1980 when my life, in my mid-twenties, pretty much blew up in my face. It was a perfect storm of stress from opening a restaurant business, unresolved issues in relationships, and issues with anxiety. When things came to a head, as they have a way of doing, I found my way first into psychotherapy, and then into a new approach of taking responsibility for my own health.

A healing journey was underway, which continues to this day. It's often challenging, sometimes terrifying, and always ultimately rewarding. As we travel through this book together, I'll share more about that journey and its unique twists and turns.

1.1 THE DAYS OF THE GP

If you jumped back 50 years in time, you'd enter a world of general practitioners and doctors still making house calls. As the name implies, your GP was a generalist, familiar with the signs and symptoms of many conditions, and was there to provide context and meaning through their personal relationship with patients.

Today there is fragmentation in the health-care system. Even if you have a doctor who makes referrals to specialists, he or she no longer functions the way the GP of old did. Various pressures in the health-care system make it very unlikely that even a dedicated doctor with the best of intentions will consistently do the following:

- Take time to really listen to your experience with your condition.
- Get a clear enough understanding of your health history to be able to take that into consideration in recommending your treatment.
- Stay abreast of the latest diagnostic and treatment options from an impartial source – one without a conflict of interest.

Even if one doctor orders various tests, the results are interpreted in a disconnected way, not in a contextual way that seeks to help you understand what it means for your blood sugar number to be high on the day you took a random test. In other words, if you take another test and the numbers are normal, no further action is needed. You're fine. Never mind.

There's no attempt to make sense of why the number went out of bounds in the first place. This is one aspect of fragmentation.

Another aspect of fragmentation is too many specialists, with not enough integration. For example, when my mother had a heart attack and went into the hospital for testing and treatment, many specialists were brought in for various aspects of her care. But no one person owned the big picture.

Increasingly, it falls to the patient to cobble together the big picture and make sense of all the fragmented information they receive. This is often true at a time when the patient is impacted emotionally by a frightening diagnosis. So at the time they need their wits about them the most, they can feel very compromised.

Therefore, many patients are more lost than ever, unless they take charge of their own health. Fortunately, more and more people are doing just that. They do research on the Internet. They seek out alternative options. They craft their own answers and solutions to health issues. This book tells their stories – and mine.

1.2 NOT ABOUT WESTERN MEDICINE VERSUS ALTERNATIVE

In the alternative health arena, it's easy to get caught up in what's "wrong" with western medicine. And as you can conclude by observing the intense pressure to "fix" our health-care system, we do have a few issues.

But to me, the dividing line is not between western medicine and alternative healing. It's between self-directed and, for lack of a better term, "other-directed" care. In my experience, you can successfully take a self-directed approach in either or both arenas. It's the self-direction that makes the difference, not the orientation of the system.

However, I'm not advocating a "do-it-yourself" approach. I believe in hiring expertise and in getting help. There's a significant difference between "do it yourself" and self-direction. Self-direction means you take the lead in your own health choices. Do-it-yourself implies that you learn to do everything yourself. In my experience with self-directed healing, I do end up learning a lot from the providers I employ, but I'm not trying to "go it alone."

The openness to self-direction is my barometer for selecting health-care providers. There are good practitioners in both western medicine and alternative fields who respect and support self-direction by their patients. There are also those in both systems who expect they will provide directions, which you will follow.

What I'm looking for, and recommend you look for, is the former; the practitioner of any stripe who is open to, and eager to embrace, my taking responsibility for my own health. I love my current chiropractor for this attribute. Even if I inadvertently hand him my power (maybe in hopes he'll "fix" me), he gently hands it right back.

1.3 It Is about a Flexible System

Even though it's more about the self-direction than the system, there are advantages to holistic over conventional methods when it comes to self-directed healing, including the following:

- **Flexibility:** Holistic health systems tend to be less entrenched in bureaucracy than their conventional counterparts. This may be partly due to conventional medicine's closer ties to the insurance industry, as well as to the business aspects of health personified by big-pharma, biotech, and the American Medical Association.
- **Collateral damage:** Holistic treatments tend to have less negative impact. Herbs, nutritional supplements, whole foods and super foods are usually closer to their natural state, and often are used in combinations that allow ingredients to work in synergy and to balance and buffer one another. Medicinal approaches usually introduce isolated and synthetic ingredients that tend to generate undesirable side effects.

- **Subtlety:** Conventional medical treatment often doesn't begin until symptoms are extreme or have progressed to serious levels. Holistic approaches sometimes have more sensitive diagnostic tools, such as applied kinesiology or the tools utilized by Traditional Chinese Medicine (TCM) practitioners, which identify imbalances that, if left untreated, would lead to illness. These tools can catch imbalances in early stages where treatments can be more subtle. It's the difference between listening to the whispers and waiting for them to become shouts.

1.4 SIGNS OF CHANGE

Even as our health-care system becomes more brittle, more fragmented and less patient-friendly, there are also positive signs of change. Holistic healthcare and alternative approaches are growing in recognition and consumer interest. Just as more and more people are buying organic foods for health reasons, more and more people are seeking alternatives to drugs and surgery.

All of the following represent new innovation, fresh air and hope for people seeking healing:

- **Integrative medicine**, such as Dr. Andrew Weil teaches at his Arizona Center for Integrative Medicine, is bridging the gap between conventional medicine and holistic approaches.
- **Holistic doctors**, such as Dr. Christiane Northrup, who focus more on "flourishing" and women's empowerment than on managing disease.
- **Alternative approaches**. The National Center for Health Statistics at the Centers for Disease Control and

Prevention estimates that nearly 40 percent of adult Americans report using some form of complementary and alternative therapies, known as CAM.

- **Functional medicine**, which "addresses the underlying causes of disease, using a systems-oriented approach and engaging both patient and practitioner in a therapeutic partnership," according to The Institute for Functional Medicine.

These are just a few of the many harbingers of change in our health and healing landscape. And they in no way detract from the resurgence of traditional healing modalities such as Herbalism, Traditional Chinese Medicine and the various energy healing methods.

They also do not diminish the medical doctors who have dedicated themselves to the healing of their patients. However, many medical doctors lack the tools and training to address preventative care beyond the so-called preventive tests that are pervasive. Most receive no or very little training in nutrition and lifestyle. And until recently, many medical recommendations were based on research that assumed that men and women were the same when it came to how medications affect them. For these reasons, I have found it wise to question medical authorities, and take charge of my own health-care decisions.

1.5 ISSUES RESOLVED WITH THIS APPROACH

Some examples of issues I've resolved using this approach (my own, my client's and the people I interviewed for this book) include the following:

- Weight gain
- Gout
- Menopausal symptoms
- Arthritis
- Digestive problems
- High cholesterol
- Allergies
- Muscle spasms
- Low back pain

- Chronic pain
- High blood pressure
- Food allergies
- Migraine headaches
- Gall bladder pain
- Sleep apnea
- Anxiety
- Vertigo

1.6 WHY MOVE AWAY FROM CONVENTIONAL HEALTHCARE?

So why are people moving away from "big healthcare"? First of all, it's dangerous.

Harm from our healthcare system causes more than 700 thousand deaths annually, costing over $200 billion annually. (See: http://www.ourcivilisation.com/medicine/usamed. htm)

Secondly, it's cumbersome. In fact, health-care systems in America are on the verge of a wave of process reengineering, due to Obamacare and industry pressures to reduce costs and streamline care. It remains to be seen whether these changes will benefit the consumer or just the big business interests.

And thirdly, it's costly. $1.5 trillion – or 15% of our gross national product – is spent on health care.

1.7 MY GOAL

My goal with this book is to formalize a process for taking charge of your own health that is:

- **Safe:** At first glance, taking responsibility for your own health-care decisions may seem a little risky, especially if you're accustomed to turning to the "experts" to tell you what to do. I'm not suggesting that you just make up whatever you want. I'm saying that with research, advice from doctors and other experts, and your own experiences with your health you are capable of making an informed decision. In fact, you are in a better position than anyone else to do that because you have more information. You have the information that comes from your own body – the organism that you are – and from beyond your conscious mind, through various channels like the body and the emotions.
- **Simple:** It's my goal to distill a simple method that anyone can follow to take charge of their own health. The seven-step process that I've developed isn't a magic formula that works no matter what. You have to make it work. But it does give you a framework of reference for doing that. It gives you cues about what to expect in your own healing journey.
- **Inexpensive:** Anyone can follow this simple method, and it doesn't cost anything extra to do so. You'll still be paying for the advice, health-care providers, and treatments that you choose. But you'll be in the lead on making those decisions. And you'll be increasingly able to discern what not to do, and what's not needed.
- **Workable:** The process is designed to start where you are and go from there. If you get lost, you can always

read through the steps and see what resonates with you to determine where to start.

- **Empowering:** One of the benefits of taking charge of your own health is that the process moves you beyond your fears, as you discover your own power. It may not happen immediately, and I don't mean to diminish the fears that can surface when it comes to your health. After all, these decisions are sometimes life-or-death. But I do assert that the safest way to address them is from an empowered place where you are in charge. Anything less seems a bit like Russian roulette.

- **Adaptable:** This process works in an inclusive and integrative way. It's not my intention to favor any particular form of health care; but rather to develop a process that works with any combination of help that you choose.

- **Navigable:** The process is a framework of reference providing the ability to make ongoing course corrections. You should expect to need corrections along the way.

I believe this process will greatly improve your odds in the health-care crisis that already is upon us, a crisis many experts say can only worsen. There is a lot of pressure on the system between the retirement of baby boomers taxing our health-care resources, and the rise of obesity-related illnesses. Personally, I'd rather not rely exclusively on the standard American health-care system. My best solution is to stay healthy, and that's my goal for you.

CHAPTER 2

~

A SIMPLE METHOD

The method I've developed is simple. It's a seven-step process that anyone can follow.

But it's not a magic bullet, and it requires much from the reader. It has some complexity to take into account, but anything else would not cover enough territory. You need to know about the complexity because it is inherent in healing.

2.1 FOUR DIMENSIONS OF HEALING

I believe that healing occurs on many levels. There are four dimensions in particular in which healing can occur and in which issues can arise. Sometimes we experience them as discrete, and sometimes they can overlap. They are as follows:

- **Physical:** Includes issues, illness, physical pain and dysfunction. Often problems manifesting on the physical level are caused by imbalances in the other three levels.
- **Emotional:** All feelings, sensing and intuition occur in this dimension. Intuition is an example of a feeling that can overlap to the other dimensions. For example, physical pain is often caused by intuition trying to make itself heard.
- **Mental:** The mental dimension includes thoughts, visions and ideas. It may be associated with the head,

eyes, and sometimes the heart.
- **Spiritual:** A dimension that goes beyond the physical, the spiritual often comes into play in healing. People experience the influence of Soul and Spirit in this dimension, and a sense of something larger than themselves.

Most people spend more time in one or two of these dimensions of healing in their process. Sometimes, part of the healing is learning to bring the four dimensions into greater balance and harmony. Or sometimes we experience a blockage in one of the dimensions and clearing that blockage is part of the healing.

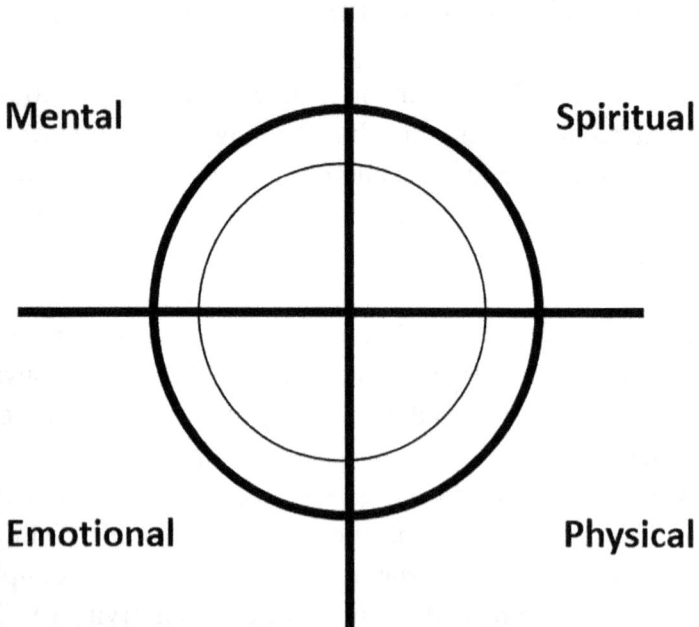

Mental   **Spiritual**

Emotional   **Physical**

Figure 2.1: Shows the four dimensions placed on a crosshairs model.

It often happens that the crosshairs don't meet in the exact middle of the four quadrants. Instead, they move around to include more of one dimension to the exclusion or reduction of focus on the others.

For example, many of us in the West spend a majority of our time in the mental sphere, confining most of our energy to our heads. The distribution of attention within the dimensions for such a person would look something like the picture in Figure 2.2.

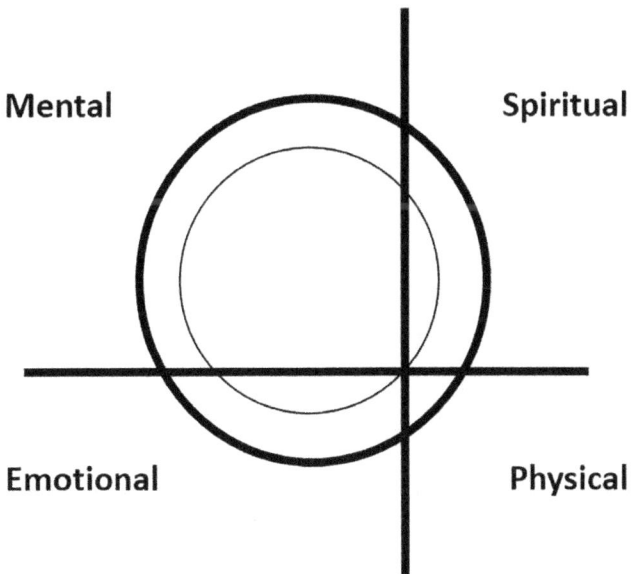

Figure 2.2: Model of a person who spends more time in the mental sphere of attention

Similarly, you could move the crosshairs around to depict a primary focus on any of the four dimensions. It's natural for personality differences to lead us to emphasize one quadrant over the others, but also a good idea to seek to find balance of all four.

2.2 SYNERGISTIC HEALING

Your life is what your thoughts make it.
            – MARCUS AURELIUS

The simple method offered in this book incorporates an approach called synergistic healing, which enables the integration of multiple approaches to healing and to a health-promoting lifestyle. Synergistic healing is an approach that integrates multiple solutions – treatments, dietary and lifestyle changes, and protocols – into a system for healing and health.

The synergistic approach operates as a road map for navigating the self-directed health landscape, from conventional western to holistic systems, to the emerging models of integrative healthcare.

This approach requires the individual to embrace and explore health issues by learning to listen to the body. It recognizes illness symptoms as messages from the body that should be explored rather than overridden. It also requires patience as synergy builds over time, and a willingness in the individual to continue to adopt new perspectives and apply new levers.

The mindset is not one of virtue, but pragmatism. Approaches that demonstrate positive results are continued, while those that don't are weeded out and replaced. It is a system of prevention in which the focus is on taking personal responsibility for health. Synergistic healing requires self-reliance and an awareness of conscious reality creation.

Bio-individuality – the recognition that one person's food is another one's poison – dictates that we learn to craft our own personal, unique solutions. The goal in each instance is to arrive at the turning point, which often occurs when the focus is off (as has been famously noted with Einstein's napping).

This integrative approach involves making subtle manipulations with treatment, herbs, supplements, and other methods aimed at supporting the organism (the body) to return to balance. Its goal is removing the pressure that's causing the imbalance, and allowing the body to right itself naturally, which is what our bodies are always working to do.

Grounded in thirty years of applied research, both personal and professional, the synergistic healing approach emerged over time as my primary method of maintaining health and wellness. It goes beyond incremental improvements to promote the transformation of one's health.

In this system, success is not finding that one special treatment. It is applying approaches synergistically until they take on a life of their own. You could say that synergistic healing is the "light twin" of drug interactions.

2.3 OPERATES AS A ROAD MAP

*This is my way. What is your way? THE way
doesn't exist.*
                    – FRIEDRICH NIETZSCHE

The simple method described in this book operates as a road
map for navigating the self-directed health landscape. The
characteristics of this road map include the following:

- **Start where you are.** This method is designed to
  meet you where you are. As with a road map, you can
  start from any point on the map that you might find
  yourself.
- **Choose your path.** It all depends on where you want
  to go. Just as with a road map, the route you choose
  for your journey will depend on your goals.
- **Multiple routes possible.** There are many ways
  to reach your destination. The choices you make will
  determine what road is best for you.

2.4 BENEFITS OF MY APPROACH

This simple method offers the following benefits:

- **An approach** that is synergistic and choice-centered
  that can be tailored by the individual depending on
  their needs and preferences.
- **Flexibility** to start where you are and chart your own
  course.
- **A road map** with "triptychs" - examples from my
  experience and those of the people I've interviewed
  who have taken charge of their own health. These

examples illuminate various routes through the terrain.

- **Tools and techniques** to follow that put you in charge of your health.
- **A simple guide** for navigating the complexities of self-directed health.

2.5 WHAT IS REQUIRED?

One doesn't discover new lands without consenting to lose sight of the shore for a very long time.

- ANDRE GIDE

This method works best when you learn to embrace and explore a healthy lifestyle whether you currently are dealing with issues or not. The way to do that is by learning to listen to your body. I don't know if we're born with the ability to listen to our bodies, but if we are, we've been trained out of it. As a holistic health coach, I teach clients that skill again, because it is a skill that you can learn.

And it's when you learn this skill that you can create a ripple effect in your own life that starts with listening to your intuition about your health choices. This will cascade out to other choices you make in life, and will bolster the energy you experience, the balance in your life, and the ease with which you go through life.

Our bodies are constantly talking to us, sending us messages about our food and other choices, our activities, and the effects of our thoughts and feelings.

It's important to learn to start listening to these messages from your body. And I'm not just talking about realizing when you're nauseous. It has many layers to it, and because each of us is unique, that will play out for each of us in our own individual manner.

But the universal truth is that when someone learns that skill they possess it for life, and their lives become better.

One of the reasons to listen to your body is that the symptoms of illness are messages from your body, to be explored, rather than overridden. In our culture, we tend to want to override our feelings, putting them on hold while we attend to the "more important" business of our daily lives. In this approach, you want to learn to "listen to the whispers," before they have the chance to become shouts.

This approach also requires patience, because synergy builds over time. Along with that, it takes a willingness to continue adopting new perspectives and applying new levers. It's perhaps harder at first, but it becomes easier as you go along.

2.6 SYNERGISTIC HEALING REQUIRES A CHANGE OF MINDSET

As far as I'm concerned, I prefer silent vice to ostentatious virtue.

— **ALBERT EINSTEIN**

The self-directed approach requires that we stop thinking of healthy ways as "virtuous," and start thinking of them as pragmatic. In other words, healthy choices are valuable because they help us to get what we want, whether that's more energy, losing weight, releasing pain or preventing or reversing chronic illness. They are not valuable because they make us "good people."

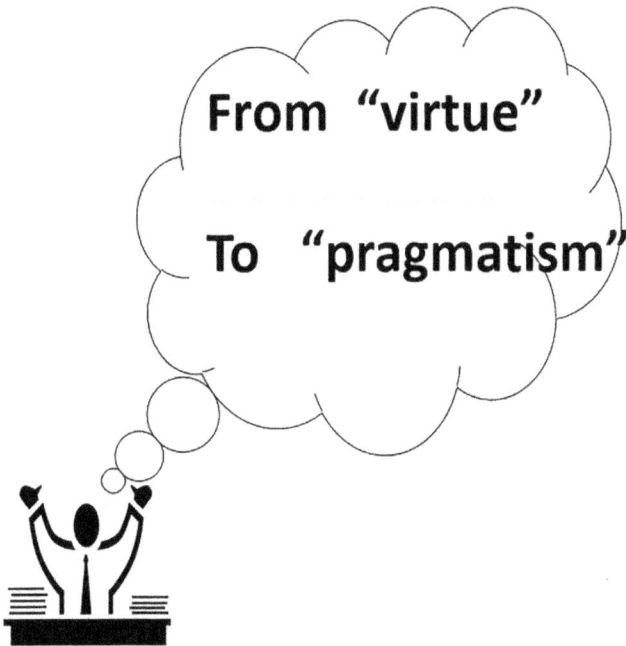

Figure 2.3: Graphic depicts the change of mindset required by the self-directed approach.

Confusing virtue with pragmatism when it comes to food and lifestyle choices can set up a very judgmental situation, one where some people even become afraid of food and hesitant to make their own choices. In fact, there's even a new phobia that's been called Cibophobia, defined as "fear of food." About.com's health phobia section has this definition: "People with this phobia are sometimes mistakenly thought to suffer from anorexia, a dangerous eating disorder. The main difference is that those with anorexia fear the effects of food on body image, while those with cibophobia are actually afraid of the food itself."

Removing the judgment is central to working effectively with your health and choices. Judgment stops movement and destroys momentum. If we can lift, or even just suspend, our judgment, it will open up our options and our understanding.

I like restraint, if it doesn't go too far.
– MAE WEST

2.7 SYNERGISTIC HEALING REQUIRES A SHIFT TO WELLNESS

The approach I'm advocating also requires that we change our thinking in the following ways:

- **From "does it work?" to "does it help?"**
  When you're pursuing synergy in your treatments, protocols and practices, what you're looking for is things that help. It can be an interesting experiment to see if you can make your symptoms worse. If you can, it shows you have the power to affect your symptoms, and if you can make them worse, you can probably make them better. So what we're looking for are things that push you in the desired direction.

  The question "does it work" suggests a magic bullet or a one-shot fix. "Does it help" suggests an ongoing process with subtle adjustments that are added in and evaluated on an ongoing basis, by listening to our bodies.

- **From "placebo effect" (i.e. not real) to "affirmation effect" (from the inside out - i.e. more real)**
  The placebo effect is considered "all in the mind"as defined by MedicineNet.com: "A remarkable phenomenon in which a placebo – a fake treatment, an inactive substance like sugar, distilled water, or saline solution – can sometimes improve a patient's condition simply because the person has the expectation that it will be helpful."

  To harness the power of the mind, we change our thinking to embrace the effects of affirmation, positive thinking and the power of expectation. This shift recognizes the fact that change occurs most deeply from the inside out. Or in other words, from the inner world, the more real world, to the outer world, the physical plane which is an illusion.

- **From "demonstrated by science" to "demonstrated in my personal bio-computer"**
  "Demonstrated by science" implies an external reference point as authority. When we learn to listen to our bodies, we gain access to a whole laboratory of our own. That lab is our personal bio-computer, which we can tune into.

  Once we do, we can learn to experiment and fine-tune our food and supplement usage, as well as the type of exercise we choose, our methods of relaxation and

other aspects of healing, based on feedback from our
bodies.

■ **From "product of my past" to "future I choose
organizes my present"**

The wellness paradigm also shifts us away from seeing
ourselves as a product of our past, which implies the
inability to go beyond where we've already been. My
definition of creativity is going beyond our current
repertoire in any given area.

Another way to express it is as free agency: Last time
I checked, I am still a free agent, free to choose, free
to decide what I will do. I am the owner of my body
and the author of my experience, not some expert. Me
myself and I. I choose, which has been very helpful in
building the health and the life that I want.

Perhaps I didn't accomplish what I set out to the first
time around. Perhaps I have been pursuing goals in
other areas of life, in order to hone the skills that will
be needed to succeed, then to return to this challenge
with new understanding. If so, I would be in good
company, for in my recent studies of the genius Leon-
ardo da Vinci, I've learned that this was his method.
He pursued multiple projects, multiple lines of inquiry.
When he learned something new on one line, he
returned to the others and applied this new learning.

I am not a product of my past. There is innovation
everywhere you look. The world moves on. I prefer
to look to my future, where the future I choose can
organize my present. For instance, I can make a choice
to lose weight over the next 3 months, say in time for

summer. If I go ahead and pick out my "skinny jeans" or a slimmer bathing suit, that choice will begin to influence my current-day decisions if I let it. I might reach for a healthy dessert or no dessert at all if I'm looking forward to wearing those summer clothes.

- **From "drug interactions" to "synergistic healing"**
  In the medical model, the threat of drug interactions exists. Taking one medication which impacts the effects of another medication can be dangerous. In the holistic model, synergistic healing relies on one treatment to enhance the effectiveness of another, until the desired results are achieved.

- **From "brute force intervention" to "balancing act"**
  Drugs and surgery, while irreplaceable when needed, are often more of a brute force intervention. For example, last spring when I got sick on vacation and didn't have access to my usual more subtle measures such as herbs, supplements and super-foods, I was pretty sick by the time I got home. I was so sick that I needed steroids and antibiotics to fight infections that had gotten established. But I know that, if I'd had my usual toolkit with me, I wouldn't have gotten as sick. And, I would have been able to regain my balance more easily. As it was, I needed a little "brute force" to get over the worst of the symptoms. But then I was still out of balance from taking the medications, and it took two or three weeks to really get back into balance using natural means.

The wellness point of view regards health as more of a

balancing act, and works to remove any stresses on the system that keep our health from returning to balance.

■ **From "illness" to "wellness and wholeness"**
Western medicine tends to define wellness as the absence of illness. In synergistic healing, the focus is on wellness and wholeness. The premise is that the background is really just as important as the foreground. In the foreground, we see illness or disease – some pathogen taking hold. But what happens in the background – the environment of our health – determines whether that pathogen or germ finds fertile ground in which to take hold. Keep the environment healthy and you can withstand attacks and conditions that would sicken a person less healthy overall.

This concept is very similar to the organic gardening goal of keeping the plants healthy by feeding the soil. Healthy plants don't attract pests and disease, and no chemical pesticides are needed. Your body, as an overall system, is your soil. It's the background environment in which your personality, your energy, the flowering of who you are grows. Healthy soil allows for the full expression of who we are capable of becoming.

■ **From "discipline of the body" to "working with our bodies"**
Synergistic healing is less about controlling ourselves, our food and Nature and more about having the best food ever, the best health we personally can achieve, and the best life. It's about working with our bodies instead of against them. When we think in terms of discipline, we fight against our bodies, seeking to overcome their supposed "weaknesses." This might

take the form of punishing exercise, or "stuffing our feelings" with food and drink.

Working with our bodies means listening to them, feeling our feelings and releasing them, then seeking to understand what's behind the symptoms. If the diabetic wants more sugar than is healthy, what is the sweetness in life they might be craving? If a person is too fond of alcohol, what is the "spirit" they are seeking? Could it be a longing for a more spiritual connection? Or if someone is craving salt, could there be a mineral imbalance at work? There's not a "direct translation" that fits everyone. The meaning behind the craving depends on what is meaningful to the individual.

- **From "majority rule" to "individual approach"**
  Have you ever noticed that it's the majority that informs medical research and drug trials? And until recently, research and drug testing utilized almost exclusively male populations, with the assumption that results would hold true for women as well. What works for the majority doesn't take into account the varied needs of individuals. The self-directed approach is the ultimate customized, tailored solution. It allows you to test and adjust as you learn exactly what works for you and your body.

- **From "doctor knows best" to "listen to your body"**
  The "doctor knows best" position assumes an external authority. It employs the model of the expert who's training in technology trumps the knowledge the individual has of the "local conditions" (i.e. our own bodies). There is a big difference between the expert

approach and an approach that respects the knowledge
and rights of the individual.

■ **From "describe your symptoms" to "read this
and see if it sounds familiar"**
This shift suggests that it's valuable to describe your
symptoms to a practitioner, but it can also be valuable
to hear or read about the experiences of others and
gain insights into our own situation.

For example, one of the women I interviewed for this
book told me the story of her problems with vertigo
and how it turned out to be migraine-related. Hearing
her story made me realize that my own experiences
with vertigo might also stem from migraine trigger
syndrome, and gave me new avenues to explore for
healing.

In summary, changing our thinking is a big part of changing
our health. To take another analogy from organic gardening, changing our thinking, or not, is like the difference
between "shallow organics" and "deep organics." also known
as "beyond organics." Shallow organics involves the same
inputs as non-organic growing: fertilizers and pesticides.
Shallow organics just uses approved substances for the fer-
tilizer and pesticide. Deep organics goes beyond that concept
and focuses on the health of the soil. In deep organics, the
healthy soil grows healthy plants that don't require fertilizers
and pesticides.

CHAPTER 3

~

SETTING UP CONDITIONS
FOR SUCCESS

My goal in this chapter is to set up the conditions that will make you most successful in taking charge of your own health. In their book *The Power of Full Engagement*, Jim Loehr and Tony Schwartz share research showing that "the limitations of conscious will and discipline are rooted in the fact that every demand on our self-control - from deciding what we eat to managing frustration ... all draw on the same small, easily depleted reservoir of energy."

Armed with this knowledge – that conscious will and discipline are limited in their effectiveness when it comes to changing our habits – we aim to create an environment of support where you are in touch with your birthright - the right to seek and find help. We also need to stay in control of our own destinies, and so this chapter addresses how to do that even in the face of systems that discourage our ownership of our own health.

And finally, this chapter is not about opposition to or rebellion against any outside authority. It is about being your own authority - empowering yourself. If that seems a daunting task right now, remember that we'll take an approach I learned from my mother about building and maintaining a garden, which she simply called "do a little along." It means you don't have to do everything at once. You don't have to make a clean sweep and turn your life upside down. And you don't have to have it all figured out before you start.

You can simply do one step at a time; do what you can when you can, and let the rest wait for another time. As you continue to return to doing "a little along," the doing will add up and before you know it you'll be in another place altogether.

3.1 Getting Help (Environment of Support)

"Rarely do members of the same family grow up under the same roof."

— **Richard Bach**

One of the women I interviewed for this book said it very well. She told me about an exercise she did at a conference called "finding your why." She thought she knew what her "why" was, but discovered in the exercise that it was not what she thought it was. "It was healing my body, and believing that you have the birthright to find someone to help you ... and if that help is costly, you have the right to use your means to pay for that cost ... because it's your birthright to heal."

So this is me encouraging you to get help, and reminding you that taking charge of your own health doesn't have to mean "going it alone." Indeed, for many people I've known who took this self-directed approach to healing, it seemed that learning to reach out and find help was itself a part of their healing. And I know that's been true for me, in my own process.

3.2 HOW TO WORK WITH HEALTH CARE PROVIDERS AND STAY IN CONTROL OF THE DIRECTION

Well behaved women rarely make history.
— LAUREL ULRICH

You need to determine whether a provider offers a closed system (all you need you'll get from me), or whether their system is open. Top-down, hierarchical systems are usually closed, even if they demand open-mindedness from you. That's not to say you can't work with a closed system, but you will have to be mindful of owning the relationship and fitting their advice and treatments into your own plan. It's not advisable to allow a provider of a closed system to own the plan for your treatment.

TOP-DOWN HIERARCHY

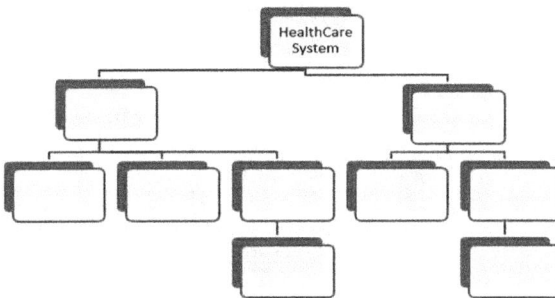

Figure 3.1:- Model of a top-down hierarchy

The top-down hierarchy is the typical organization found with the western approach to healthcare. At the top are doctors, often with hospital administrators and/or insurance companies over them and influencing their decisions.

The patient, in this model, often appears in one of the bottom boxes, under the authority of the health-care providers above.

In my corporate work, I was introduced to the concept of the relational model, which supports non-hierarchical organization. In that setting, the relational concept was applied to business data. People figured out that data tends to change and grow over time, and it is easier to maintain it when you don't have to go all the way to the top of the chart to change one little item at a lower level.

So the relational model was developed which allowed easier maintenance, and captured the relationships between entities.

RELATIONAL MODEL

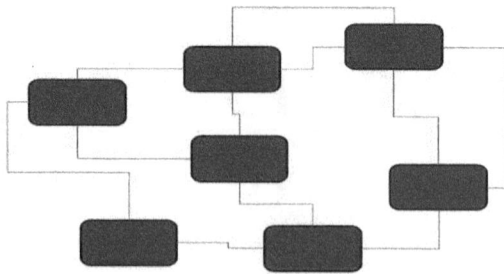

Figure 3.2: Model of a relational organization model

The shift to the relational model allows for the more open system shown above. For example, say I see a provider in a closed system, such as a medical center that has its own nutritionist, radiologist and anesthesiologist, and maybe a physical therapist, and so forth. If I decided to make a change, I would most likely be leaving behind all the resources located there – those in the top box, and all the boxes under it on the diagram. Then I would have to find a new "top box," and get connected with all the resources in that hierarchy.

The relational model would allow me to make or break connections with providers one at a time, without having some of the resources dependent upon the top of the pyramid. You could also call this relational model a network. Not like an "in-network" versus and "out of network" provider, for that still implies top-down control. But as in nodes and connections, where any node can connect to, or find a path to connect to, any other node, much like the way the Internet operates.

Variations

Some providers will operate as a hybrid of closed and open. Some will be operating within an open system, which doesn't require adherence to its own principles exclusively.

When the system is closed, information will tend to be lopsided, fragmented and incomplete. It's up to us to knit the pieces together into a coherent point of view. That's because the closed system is dependent upon one pyramid. Gathering multiple points of view builds perspective.

We need to understand the difference between the western

medicine model of illness – you're well when you're not sick – and that of the self-directed approach.

In the self-directed approach, we make subtle manipulations with treatments, herbs, supplements aimed at supporting the body to return to balance. It's about removing the pressure that's causing the imbalance, and allowing the body to right itself naturally, which is what our bodies are always working to do.

In the western model, it's like using a sledge hammer: Drugs and surgery delivering immediate results, but often making the underlying condition worse. For example, in the case of my allergies to pine pollen, the drugs became a bigger problem than the condition. And the increasing doses required to achieve the same results put pressure on my liver, which is also in charge of the sinuses.

In other words, it became a vicious cycle of more drugs impacting the liver, making it work less well, and then needing more drugs to control symptoms.

Another example of covering up the symptoms without treating underlying causes is in digestive problems. If you have low stomach acid and take antacids, as I discovered with my own health, you are making the underlying cause of the symptoms worse.

The symptoms of low stomach acid mimic the symptoms of too much acid and are often misdiagnosed as an ulcer, as in my case. Then the treatments that reduce stomach acid just make matters worse.

3.3 Having a Plan of Your Own

Inside me lives a skinny woman trying to get out. I can usually shut the bitch up with cookies.

– Author unknown

It can be helpful to remember that the experts don't own you or your health. You are your own best expert. The parties best equipped to make the decisions are the parties most affected by those decisions.

It's important to develop a plan for your treatment-recovery-wellness. This plan can be sketchy or it can be deep and detailed; you just need to have one. Because if you don't have a plan, you will be tempted to follow along with someone else's plan. Bad idea.

What you really want to do is partner with your health-care providers. Sometimes the tricky bit is getting them to partner back. The best thing you can do is to act like an equal partner, take your time, and focus on what YOU need, and what YOU know.

My action plan is sometimes not all on paper, with some parts of it only in my head. But it's pretty detailed. For example, my plan includes the following:

- Nutritional supplements I'm planning to take
- Dietary changes
- Super foods
- Herbs and herbal teas
- Exercise and movement, such as Qi Gong, Yoga, back

strengthening exercises, posture improvements, stretching and walking

- Any practitioners I'll involve such as chiropractor, massage therapist, acupuncturist
- I also might have a list of rituals that I've learned will help me change my habits, or help me choose how I intend to feel
- And there will be some idea of the supports I need or have, such as a support group, an informative online community I've found, an accountability partner, a holistic health coach
- Rituals that support the changes I'm making. For example, I used to get anxious before taking a trip or vacation. I've developed rituals of packing and planning that I do the same way every time I travel and it serves two purposes. The ritual reduces anxiety that I might forget something, because I use the same checklist every time. It also reduces anxiety because once I get into the ritual, it feels familiar and comfortable.
- I would have an idea of a set of goals, if only 2 or 3 things I plan to implement in the next 2 weeks. I use these to evaluate progress and make additions or adjustments.

The action plan develops over time. The idea is not to launch a revolution, but to build over time, making small changes and testing them out over two or three weeks and then adding in further changes for a cumulative effect. It can be helpful to keep a log or diary that includes your plan, the current treatments and how they are working. See the appendix for a sample action plan and template.

You might want to keep your own health records, logs, diary and statistics about your health, and share as you feel it's appropriate with health-care providers. I recommend erring on the side of caution when it comes to giving health-care providers your entire health history, especially when it comes to online questionnaires. It's a matter of privacy as well as security. Security experts in the computer business will tell you the safest way to keep records on a computer is to have it completely disconnected from the Internet. No phone lines, no modem. Just be thoughtful about how much information you give out, and be aware of how it's being stored, and with whom it may be shared.

3.4 THE BEST DOCTORS-PROVIDERS WANT THEIR CLIENTS TO DO THIS

The best doctors and health-care providers want and expect their patients to take an active role in their recovery. They welcome your questions and knowledge of your own body.

For example, I used to see a chiropractor who was very popular and successful. I thought he could really help me, but I was sometimes bothered by the fact that he just wasn't a good listener. He was a talker, and a bit of a self-promoter. He liked to control the conversation, and keep it going in his direction.

It wasn't until I was in so much pain that I finally looked for a new chiropractor that I realized perhaps this one wasn't serving me. The new chiropractor totally respected my knowledge of my own body, my needs and really listened anytime I spoke. What a difference that makes! This doctor has the humility and the courage to let his patients take the lead.

That's the kind of doctor you want to find: one who honors your wisdom, your intuition and your knowledge.

Incidentally, I don't feel that the chiropractor who didn't listen well had anything other than a desire to support me in my healing. I know he cared about me and respected me. His style just wasn't conducive to my needs. The situation taught me that it's my job to honor my needs as I determine the style of doctoring I accept.

3.5 IT'S NOT ABOUT OPPOSITION OR REBELLION AGAINST ANY OUTSIDE AUTHORITY

The self-directed approach is not about opposition to doctors, western medicine or any outside authority. Opposition and rebellion have a way of defining you.

You just do the opposite of what you're told. That's not empowering.

I learned that lesson when I learned to let go of rebelling against my mother's control.

For years I'd been seeing myself as this rebel without a cause, this radical individualist, when really all along I'd been defining myself by comparison to my mother.

It was only when I learned to use an internal reference point – my own feelings and desires regardless of what others think – that I found the freedom to carve out my own way.

3.6 IT IS ABOUT BEING YOUR OWN AUTHORITY - EMPOWERING YOURSELF

On the other hand, self-directed healing is about becoming your own authority. To do that, you want to enhance the relationship between the mind and the body. For example, it's my intention, when working with a health coaching client, that one not dictate to the other, so the mind is not telling the body what to eat based on some list of good and bad foods while, at the same time, the body is not driving you to eat from that "more, more" place that we can all get into.

But rather, that the mind and body are engaged with each other as in a conversation. As a holistic health coach, I try to facilitate that conversation. It's something you can learn to do on your own, this engaging in conversation with your body. And it's the basis for your empowerment with your health.

3.7 A LITTLE ALONG

As I mentioned in the introduction to this section of the book, my mother taught me this style of working she called "do a little along." And I've adapted it to many situations, to keep down the feelings of overwhelm, and work in an easy, results-accumulating fashion.

It's amazingly effective. Whatever you're working on grows in an organic way, building over time. It reminds me of what my financial planner calls "dollar cost averaging," where you make regular, periodic contributions to your 401k, allowing you to take best advantage of fluctuations in price in the stock market. It's the regular periodic contributions that add up over time.

And okay, it doesn't mean your holdings can never be wiped out in a stock market crash, just like your health can sometimes take a downturn. But it puts you in an advantaged position. As Gregory, an English entrepreneur once told me when I was driving across the country in my Volkswagen bug and he was speaking of safety: "play the odds, Love, always play the odds." That's what we're doing here. We're improving our odds in the long run.

PART II

~

STEPS OF THE METHOD

In this part, I'll introduce each of seven steps of the method for taking charge of your own health. Each step is viewed from four dimensions, or perspectives, of healing: physical, emotional, mental and spiritual. Particular attention is paid to the emotional dimension, because it's often a stumbling block and a significant lever to utilize. Any dimension can play either a positive or negative role in healing.

Principles to keep in mind:

■ **Synergistic healing creates an unstoppable force.** Healing modalities applied synergistically can add up to exponential improvement. My favorite illustration of this concept is to imagine a pool where lily pads grow. Exponential growth means the lily pads grow to double their coverage of the pool - let's say every week. On week one, the pads are covering a small ¼ of the pool. On week two, they cover half. Still seems like a relatively small amount. On week three, they cover the whole pool. That leap from half coverage to full coverage that happens in one week is the exponential effect.
The power isn't in finding that one special treatment. It's in the approach of applying treatments

synergistically and not stopping until you've achieved the desired healing. In the alternative health world, synergistic healing is the "light twin" of drug interactions in the western medical model.

- **Embracing and exploring issues.** We need to learn to embrace the signals coming from our bodies, rather than running from them or trying to control them. Your body is sending you messages. Don't shut them up or tune them out. Listening to your body is one of the keys to self-directed healing.
- **Patience and the willingness to suspend your disbelief and try one more thing.** This is similar to that point in adult relationships where two people are polarized in disagreement. If you can find it in yourself to just give an inch by trying to listen and understand the other's point of view (even though you're angry, etc.), that is the inch that makes relationships work. It's the difference between having a wonderful working relationship and having it all fall apart. That is similar to the feeling of being willing to suspend disbelief and try one more thing.
- **A lifestyle oriented toward wellness.** This simple method is not just for issues, but also applies to prevention, heading off genetic predispositions, and preventing the expression of genetic weaknesses. It can become a way of life, a lifestyle oriented toward wellness. In fact, the healthiest people I know practice a wellness lifestyle.
- **Taking personal responsibility for your own health.** When you learn to take personal responsibility for your own health, everything changes. That's where the power is. It's also about self-reliance and understanding how reality-creation works. I advocate

adopting the belief that I create my own (health) reality. Even if you don't believe this completely – or at all – it's still a valuable position from which to consider your life because it puts you in the most empowered position.

THE SIMPLE METHOD

~

A SEVEN-STEP PROCESS

A Simple 7 Step Process

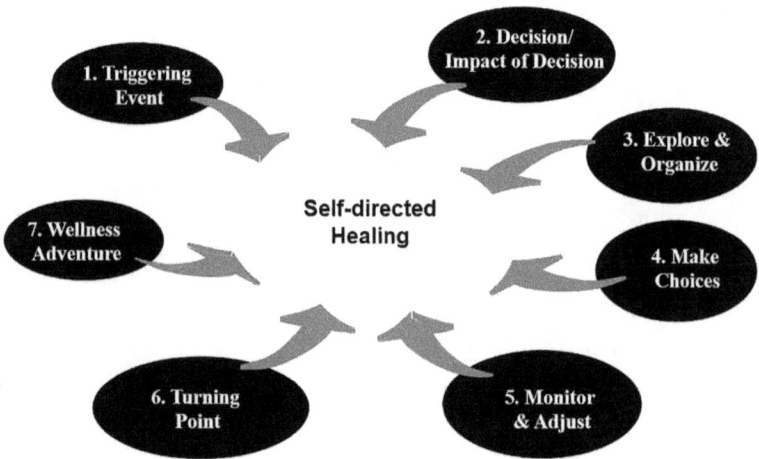

Figure II.1: The seven steps of the self-directed healing process.

The self-directed healing process usually starts with some kind of triggering event. The event may be a diagnosis, an occurrence that gets our attention, or the recognition of a state of affairs we can no longer tolerate.

The next step is when we make a decision to "do this on my own," taking charge of our health in a new way. This step also includes dealing with the impact of our decision, whether positive or negative, and the impact on those around us.

The third step is when we start to explore and get ourselves organized. We might be doing research on the Internet to look for answers, or we might be reading books and talking to experts. We might also be seeking out referrals to practitioners. It's a time of gathering information and ideas.

In step four, we start to make some choices about our direction. We look at how we intend to feel, and consider changes to our diet and lifestyle we might need to make. We might reach out to friends, groups and professionals for support in this step.

Step five is the ongoing monitoring and adjusting of our treatments, changes and approaches. It's here that we begin to notice synergies between treatments, changes and protocols, and often become more comfortable with the process we've begun. Some people report being in a positive frame of mind from the beginning.

In step six, we often experience a turning point, where the emotions go from mostly negative to mostly positive. In my experience, this is when I start to get some traction, seeing that the choices I make can make me feel better or worse. It's the point where I start to feel empowered in my health decisions. And at this point, I have an inner knowing that I'm going to succeed.

The last step is what I like to call the Wellness Adventure stage. It's when the journey has turned into an exciting adventure and all the changes I've made, the help I've found, and the choices and decisions become something greater.

This stage is characterized by feelings of gratitude, a desire to give back, and the sense of connection to something greater than us.

As we walk through the seven steps of the process in the upcoming chapters, we'll go into more detail on each, covering the four dimensions mentioned above, and exploring how these have unfolded in my experience and in the journeys of healing that our interviewees describe.

While I wanted to keep the identity of people making specific comments confidential, I do want you to hear from them in their own words. So I've included many of their remarks verbatim, except for grammatical corrections and minor clean up, as a way to illustrate how people experience these steps or phases of their own healing journeys.

STEP 1 ～ TRIGGERING EVENT

Heroes take journeys, confront dragons and
discover the treasure of their true selves.

— CARROL PEARSON

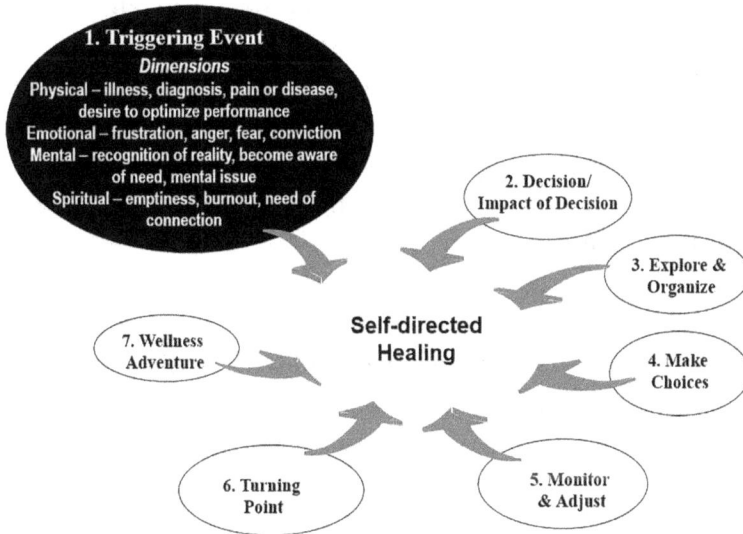

1. Triggering Event
Dimensions
Physical – illness, diagnosis, pain or disease, desire to optimize performance
Emotional – frustration, anger, fear, conviction
Mental – recognition of reality, become aware of need, mental issue
Spiritual – emptiness, burnout, need of connection

2. Decision/ Impact of Decision

3. Explore & Organize

Self-directed Healing

7. Wellness Adventure

4. Make Choices

6. Turning Point

5. Monitor & Adjust

Figure II.2: The model calls out the Triggering Event and the ways it impacts all four dimensions, physical, emotional, mental and spiritual.

The self-directed healing journey usually starts with some kind of triggering event, which may be a diagnosis, an occurrence that gets our attention, or recognition of a state of affairs we can no longer tolerate.

In my case, there had been a history of various ailments that, at the time in the 1970s, western medicine didn't have good answers for – in some cases, still doesn't. I'd had digestive issues as a child, which worsened after I had pneumonia at 10 years old and took two long rounds of antibiotics over several weeks. It would be many years later that I made the connection between the antibiotics and my digestive issues.

When the digestive problems and the pain they caused became severe in my early twenties, I was misdiagnosed with an ulcer, and advised to take the over-the-counter remedy Maalox. It was a long five years before I learned that the real problem was not too much stomach acid, but too little. After discovering that, it was a simple matter of supplementing the stomach acid, which corrected what had been an extremely painful condition.

Other issues, like allergies to pollen in the Spring that were getting worse and responding less to medication, even though the medications were increased and another one added, were also not being addressed by conventional medicine.

I'd also been plagued by anxiety since my teens. There was a time when Valium, the Xanax of the 1970s, was my answer. Valium was my substitute for all the courage, the confidence, the outgoingness I never thought I had and was always told I should possess. It was my protector and my constant companion. I never wanted to be without it again.

Of course, as you might guess, though I loved what it did for me, Valium was not really my friend. The more Valium I took, the more I needed to take to achieve the same blissful calm.

And over time, I failed to learn how to deal with situations.

Things that should have come intuitively didn't, as the drugs blocked the very pathway through which my intuition was speaking to me – my anxiety.

In my 26th year, known as the year of the "Saturn return,"a time of life when people are called to wake up and come to grips with reality, I began a healing journey to discover non-pharmaceutical approaches to dealing with both stress and anxiety. On this journey were many stepping stones.

I found many different approaches that worked, from creative visualization and "intensive journaling," to meditation and metaphysics, to Qi Gong and yoga. I learned a lot from practitioners of Traditional Chinese Medicine, Chiropractic and Kinesiology.

Having studied eastern philosophies in university before going on to study phenomenology and existentialism, I was familiar with the philosophical underpinnings of many of these practices from Taoism, Zen, Confucianism and other schools of thought.

I found a good chiropractor who also practiced the diagnostic method of kinesiology. She was the one who explained how low stomach acid was causing digestive issues. What struck me at the time was that I hadn't even mentioned digestive problems to her. I'd given up mentioning them to doctors because I knew there was nothing they could do. She picked it up with her muscle testing – the diagnostic method applied in kinesiology – and told me I'd had a lot of digestive issues. I concurred.

For me, life had become intolerably painful, and I recognized it as a state of affairs I could no longer accept.

However, it's not always an event relating to our own health that gets us started on a healing journey. I spoke to one woman who was a registered nurse, working in a hospital setting early in her career, who told me she started researching alternative healing because she could see that much of what the hospital did with poor food choices, or drugs that treated symptoms instead of seeking cures would not bring about true healing in the patients in her care.

Her "very first patient had suffered his second or third heart attack, and I knew what I was doing was not going to be healing, like the food I was required to feed him, with pats of margarine on instant mashed potatoes, pressed chicken, and canned gravy. It was disgusting! At that time in hospitals, it was still common to take patients outside to smoke a cigarette, and I took him out to smoke, removed his oxygen so he could smoke, then put it back." Soon after that, she started learning about healing with herbs and food.

She reported feeling "anger at them feeding us this line, and frustration with the system, knowing it wasn't healing but not knowing where to go from there." But once she let those feelings go, she started meeting people in all kinds of healing arts, started eating better herself and found it "amazing how you feel great. As my contacts evolved, making connections with people who "get" healing, they're just deep people who have a connection with spirituality, and you feed off of that. It's a learning journey, and you want that energy that these people have."

Another interviewee told me that "before there was a diagnosis, there was a big shift in my comfort level with my own life. I was 37 years old, and had been working in the stressful world of sales and marketing for 17 years. Right after 911 happened, I starting asking what kind of difference I'm making in the world. I decided to become a massage therapist (a decision that was a whole journey in itself). I wanted to have more of a one-on-one connection with people. So I went from sitting in a chair, not using my body much, to depending on my body to work in order to make a living.

"I started to understand, even though I was always active, that I really needed to kick it up to another level with my exercise. I built the massage practice to a full time level. About six years in, I started to have tension in my hands, along with swelling and it was very uncomfortable and scary. I'm grateful to say that I got pretty quickly to a diagnosis – it only took two to three months to get to a diagnosis of rheumatoid arthritis. That part was pretty painless for me. I also had tremendous fatigue. My hands and knees hurt. I had lots of little pain spots. But there was also this crushing fatigue. I was 43 years old."

When I asked about the emotional side of her diagnosis, she told me "I felt like I had to embark on this whole new educational endeavor. I felt very burdened by having to learn everything. Usually I'm learning because I want to and I'm excited about it, but this time I had to. It was frustrating to be forced into that. It was scary because I see from my mother's experience with RA, if I don't get this under control, I see what can happen. It's pretty terrifying."

One woman told me that it was "a number of health things, not just one" that got her started taking charge of her own health. "For most of my thirties, I'd say from age 34 on, I was very ill. I had a nodule on my thyroid that could have been cancer, one on my lung, autoimmune issues and slipped rib syndrome. With all that was going on, I was told by doctors there was no cure, just drugs to manage the condition. My health was going downhill fast, and I was not healing, just masking the symptoms."

For her, the "emotional aspect was huge, my marriage got traumatic. I was in the hospital for lung surgery, having part of my lung taken out and the nurse on duty looked at my chart and thought there must be a mistake. She thought I was 73 instead of 37 years old. She thought someone must have reversed the numbers. It was shocking, and it scared me."

As you can see, there are many different ways that people come to the decision to take charge of their own health. For one woman I interviewed, it was as simple as "I had a friend who lived the 'organic life' and she taught me." But the similarities are there. For most, there is a moment of clarity, a moment of truth, when they realize it's up to them, and they are their own best expert. Or they need to become that.

The Dimensions:

- **Physical:** *Illness, diagnosis, pain or disease, desire to optimize performance*
  In the physical dimension, the triggering event is often an illness, a diagnosis, some type of pain or disease, or even just a desire to improve your health or performance and take it to the next level. It can range from mild symptoms that we are tired of tolerating, to life-threatening illness or debilitating pain.

  Sometimes the event is definitive and clearly delineated. Sometimes it's gradual and a result of accumulated tensions, ongoing illness and a desire to be truly well. In fact, true wellness can be the siren call that motivates us to step it up a notch and really resolve our health challenges.

I know in my experience, there have been points throughout my life where I realized that my problems weren't getting any better, and I needed to dig in deeper and find new solutions. Often, that realization was the beginning of a new phase in my ongoing journey with my health.

■ **Emotional**: *Frustration, anger, fear, conviction*
The emotions involved during the triggering event can be intense. A serious diagnosis can be a frightening event, and depending on how the news is delivered, can feel like a life sentence. And if you do Internet research when immersed in fear and confusion, it can sometimes be overwhelming and make matters worse. It's like reading a medical text on all the ailments available. You may think you've got them all!

Or we may just be getting really fed up and frustrated with medical testing that doesn't yield a diagnosis, or gives a diagnosis with word that there is no cure. That's an interesting statement to me. I've come to believe that "no cure" means something more like "I don't know how to cure it, so I'm sure nobody does." When you hear those words, I recommend a little healthy skepticism.

The triggering event can also feel like a gathering conviction that it's time to take stock and make some serious changes. It may come in response to ineffectual treatments or diagnosis, or it may just be that you're getting tired of lingering ailments and annual colds.

- **Mental**: *Recognition of reality, becoming aware of need, a mental issue*
  In the dimension of our thoughts, we may experience a sense that the fog is lifting, or clouds are clearing, and we see clearly the reality of our circumstances. Or we may be becoming aware of a particular need for the first time.

  The interesting thing about thoughts is that they give rise to feelings, just as feelings give us something to think about. So it's to be expected that these dimensions will interact and influence each other.

  It's also possible that the problem or issue that triggers a decision to take charge of our own health and seek out answers is a mental issue of some kind. Indeed, healing can be needed on the level of all or any of the dimensions, and it's not uncommon for healing to encompass all four.

- **Spiritual**: *Emptiness, burnout, a need for connection*
  In the spiritual dimension, it's often a sense of emptiness or lack of connection that brings us to seek healing. It can be experienced as burnout or long-term chronic stress that leaves us feeling shell-shocked. Or sometimes, the impetus to improve our lives feels like a nudge from our Soul or Spirit. For example, when I was in my twenties, and knew my life needed changing, I had a vision one day, a sort of waking dream, where I saw myself return to my home town (I'd been living in a resort town for three years), get into therapy and totally change my life.

  In less than a year, that vision was realized. Not only

did I get into therapy, but I soon joined a community of like-minded people that became my spiritual family for the next 25 years and endures to this day.

STEP 2 ~ DECISION AND IMPACT OF DECISION

Trust yourself. Think for yourself. Act for yourself. Speak for yourself. Be yourself. Imitation is suicide.

– MARVA COLLINS

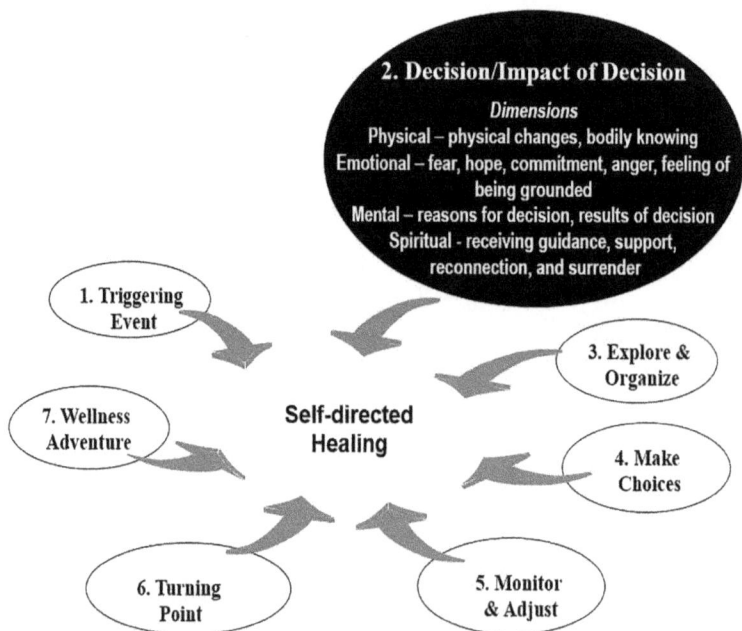

Figure II.3: The model calls out the Decision/Impact of Decision step and the ways it impacts all four dimensions, physical, emotional, mental and spiritual.

After the triggering event, we come to a decision that we are going to take charge, and do whatever it takes to heal ourselves. This decision itself often has an impact on us and on our family and friends, which should be taken into account.

One woman said: "For me, feeling sick is an incredible loss of control. That sets you off your center. Even just making small changes and starting to figure stuff out, makes me feel like okay, okay, the disease isn't in control, the doctors aren't in control. It's up to me and my body."

Another interviewee reported that what made her want to take responsibility for her own health "came as the culmination of all these (illnesses) added up over a few years. My husband thought I'd be dead by 40. My children were young. My son was six, and I remember looking at him while he was sleeping, not knowing if I'd be there for him. My daughter was only 2."

"After surgery and prednisone" she continued, "I needed to go away, and be around strong powerful women. I had the feeling I'd lost my power and my voice. I went to Costa Rica on a retreat. Four of the women there were all graduates from the Institute for Integrative Nutrition (IIN) – (a school she later enrolled in). One night we were outside on a moonlit deck, sharing our stories, and when it came my turn to share I just fell apart. My spiritual journey was huge, learning how emotions and thoughts affect our health. I wasn't spiritual before all this. I was anti-religion. Deepak Chopra's book, *The Seven Laws of Spiritual Success*, changed a lot for me. After the Costa Rica trip, I went to an ashram."

Another woman told me that she had "struggled with painful periods since age 12. At 17 years old, I started taking birth control pills and continued until I was 27. At that point, I got off the pill, and things got worse. I was in pain for 3 weeks out of the month. I'd complained to doctors about the pain for years, but it was shrugged off, and I was told to take ibuprofen. It was a coworker that mentioned endometriosis." She researched it, and got involved with a women's support group focused around endometriosis. "I was feeling written off as normal even though I knew intuitively there was more to it."

This woman found that "standard western medicine did not offer a lot of good choices of treatment. It was either birth control or hormones. I said no to both of those. That's when I discovered food as medicine, which was huge."

When she made her decision to find her own way, the shifts she experienced were "pretty dramatic, as food is very impactful. I cut out all inflammatory foods, which was a big 'outside the box' choice. I had to learn how to stand up for myself."

At the time of this writing, it's been more than 3 months since she made that decision, and "it's still a struggle at social events." When it comes to friends and family, "the biggest reaction is in them, not in me. Some others seemed almost defensive about their choices around me. You have to learn how to fend for yourself."

In my personal experience, the decision to heal myself often has immediate impacts on me. This has occurred more than once in my life, as we'll explore in future steps. It's a feeling of putting a stake in the ground and taking a stand. I may be sick and miserable, but I'm not going to take it anymore.

One of the main feelings is relief. Finally, someone's going to do something about this pain I'm in. Even if it's me doing it. In fact, I'm the one most equipped to do something.

The Dimensions:

- **Physical**: *Physical changes, bodily knowing*
  During the second step where we make a decision and experience the impact of that decision, there is sometimes immediate feedback from our bodies. Feeling physically less tense, more at ease, or having a sense of knowing, deep in your gut, that you're on the right track are common.

  For myself, I often can feel in my stomach either a tense ball or a softening that gives me feedback. I've also learned to let my physical reactions help me understand and identify my feelings. Issues like anxiety often show up in physical symptoms, often around the mid-section, where we are "processing" feelings. Sometimes when the decision has been made, I can feel that floating anxiety drop like a cloak falling to the floor.

- **Emotional**: *Fear, hope, commitment, anger, sense of being grounded*
  Many of the impacts from making a decision occur on the emotional level. Sometimes the fears increase or are just starting to arrive. I remember when I decided to attend the Institute for Integrative Nutrition, a huge healing journey for me. My anxiety arrived about a month after I made the decision, and showed up as migraine headaches driven by elevated blood pressure. Guess what health issues I worked on with my health coach for the first few months of my schooling at IIN?

There were many messages in those feelings and symptoms. One acupuncturist said to me "you need to bring your energy down." I learned that as a business technology professional and a writer, I tend to live in my head. I tend to get my energy stuck in my head, and I literally need to work to bring that energy down into my body. I do that with Qi Gong and yoga, as well as walking, swimming and gardening. I also use visualization to imagine the energy flowing down into my body and clearing away tension as it flows.

Another message from the anxiety was that the experience offered by IIN was something I needed emotionally. Have you ever noticed that sometimes, when you get close to filling a need, everything escalates? All your symptoms, your resistance pops up as if to say "turn back before it's too late." This is one way to know when you're really on track. For me, the need was to find a way to soften my exterior shell, so that I could more easily reach out to other people, and people could more easily get through to me. My experiences at IIN managed to facilitate that process of softening.

Sometimes we experience a sense of hope, or a sense of grounding in our newfound commitment to our health.

It's also not uncommon for anger to show up at this step. It's kind of like when your partner wanders off and you fear they won't come back. Until they do, you're mostly afraid. But when they do come back, and your fears subside, anger can surface and be expressed in the newly created safety.

Similarly, the initial triggering event can be so

impactful that the feelings surrounding it are all we know. Then, as we make a decision and move on, other feelings that were in the background can surface.

For me, the feelings at this stage have also included fears and intimidation focused around contradicting the authorities. These can be extreme, as in feeling that you might die if you don't follow your doctor's instructions. And sometimes the doctors are telling you just that!

Or these feelings can be akin to breaking the law by disregarding doctor's orders. (By the way, I'm not recommending disregarding your doctor's orders; just sharing with you how it can feel if that's what you decide is right for you.)

- **Mental**: *Reasons for decision, results of decision*
  On the thinking dimension, we're often recognizing the reasons we made the decision, or anticipating the results of our decision. We may be thinking about the likely outcomes, or planning our next steps.

  When I made the decision to heal my low back pain, my thoughts went to wondering whether it was even possible to heal it completely. I remembered that beliefs are a choice, and I decided I could choose to believe that, yes, it is completely possible to heal my low back pain. One of the people interviewed for this book calls that "claiming your birthright" to be healed.

- **Spiritual**: *Receiving guidance, support, reconnection, and surrender*
  It's not unusual to start receiving guidance once a

decision is made. It's like sending up a flare to your Higher Self: I'm here! And I could use some help! And this time I really mean it!!!

One of my favorite quotes is by Machaelle Wright, founder of Perelandra, and it relates to engaging with the Nature Spirits in a garden: "opening a new garden is like ringing a gong in the Devic Kingdoms" it attracts devas and nature spirits from all around to join in. Similarly, when we make a decision to heal ourselves, it attracts resources and people to help our journey.

Until one is committed
There is hesitancy, the chance to draw back
Always ineffectiveness.
Concerning all acts of initiative (and Creation)
There is one elementary truth
The ignorance which kills countless ideas and splendid plans:
That the moment that one definitely commits one's self
Then Providence moves too.
All sorts of things occur to help one
That would never otherwise have occurred.
A whole stream of events issues from the decision
Raising in one's favor all manner
Of unforeseen incidents and meetings
And material substance
Which no one could have dreamt
Would have come your way.

Whatever you can do or dream you can, begin it.
Boldness has genius, power and magic in it.
                          – William Hutchison Murray

Sometimes we experience this second stage of decision-making and impact as a sense of surrender to something greater than ourselves. By having the honesty to admit we have an issue, we are making way for a resolution.

STEP 3 ~ EXPLORE & ORGANIZE

There are three kinds of men: The one that learns by reading. The few who learn by observation. The rest of them have to pee on the electric fence for themselves.

– WILL ROGERS

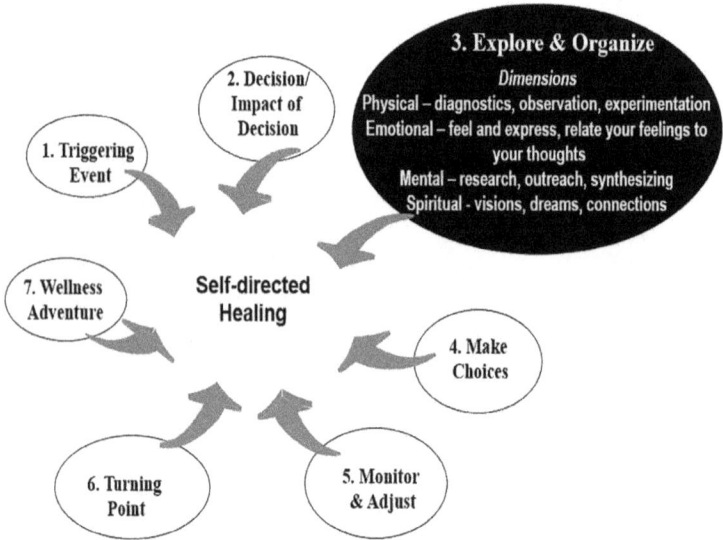

Figure II.4: The model calls out the Explore & Organize step and the ways it impacts all four dimensions, physical, emotional, mental and spiritual.

The third step is when we start to explore and get ourselves organized. We've had our moment of truth, and we've decided to strike out on our own. This is the point where we start looking for answers, and adjusting our questions as we learn. And we start to ask for help. Sometimes on the mundane levels, such as finding support groups and getting referrals to practitioners. Sometimes on the more spiritual levels, where we may find we have visions, or dreams that give us a new sense of connection.

We might be doing research on the Internet, looking for answers, or we might be reading books and talking to experts. Some people say they find inspiration in the strangest of places, as their Soul and Spirit touch their lives in mysterious, but often guiding, ways.

In fact, one woman I interviewed recounts that "right before I met my life coach, I was working on a project for an author client, a book about the Soul's plan for your life. The author was interviewing spiritual guides doing Akashic records readings of people who had unusually traumatic life experiences, and were working on whether they planned them in pre-life planning." She felt that without this experience of working with the author, she would never have been open to some of the things she heard from her life coach later on. It was as if her Soul was preparing her to open up.

It's a time of gathering information and ideas and beginning to test the waters of what works for us and what doesn't. At this point we often start making connections that will stay with us and guide the course of our journey.

The woman we heard from earlier who had a diagnosis of RA says of this time: "A couple of people had come into my life fairly close to my RA diagnosis that also have RA. That was more like, it was nice to have someone to call and talk to about stuff. One of them gave me the referral to the rheumatologist. I also got involved in quite a supportive online community where I used Twitter to connect to a bunch of people that were really strangers to me. At that point I was on Twitter all the time, which made a huge difference."

Another woman told me she found "healing people. When you open your door to that energy, people find you, sometimes in the strangest places. I had no idea what Reiki was (an energy healing practice), but a teacher I worked with introduced me to his mother, saying she does this voodoo thing I think it will help your knees. She (the mother) did a treatment on me. The energy buzzing through my body was crazy. I had to find out what this was and how to do it for other people."

One interviewee shared that "20 years ago, doctors were gods to me. That started to really shift around the time I was diagnosed with kidney disease. I started researching and having a growing awareness of drug companies and their influence on our health system. I had to stand up for my baby around not believing in getting vaccines, and I decided I should also stand up for myself."

Another woman said "a women's support group I found helped a lot. I found blogs about endometriosis (that she suffered from), and about diet. There was one blogger with a good Facebook support group based on natural healing. It was invaluable having other women who understand, especially about what it's like having chronic pain. For me, a big part of my healing is turning within, listening within. I have to pay attention. I need to listen to myself."

One interviewee made changes for her whole family. She says "Well, my husband had huge problems with acid reflux (took Tums as if it was candy). I had problems with sinus infections, reoccurring about 3-4 times a year. Our kids were always "stuffed" and the youngest had ear infections, one after another. After we made the dietary changes, things changed and we began to see a difference. So, it was a gradual change for us – one step at a time, but you could witness the results."

"My husband was the driving force at times, and the kids just had to follow along. For the most part, they were really good about not being picky with the food change. Small steps at a time..."

"Initial changes were not always easy" she continued "For example, I am from Germany. We eat a lot of cold cuts and meat. Well, when we decided as a family to not eat cold cuts anymore, the change was huge. It was the same with dairy. Now we are dairy free, but it is a constant journey."

"At first, I was pretty defensive. My holistic health coach told me in our first session that I needed to get off milk and any types of animal products. It was just too big of a step for me to take at once – and I am not sure if I will ever be vegan again. We ended up trying it as a family for 6-7 months and included Gluten-free as well. By now, I can see changes in my energy level as soon as I eat, for the better or worse. Our bodies are sensitized ... "

For me, this step is the beginning of seeing the light returning. It may just be glimmers here and there, and not fully grown at all. But it's there at least some of the time. I enjoy the exploration and it gives me hope. And getting organized always makes me feel more in charge.

The Dimensions:
- **Physical**: *Diagnostics, observation, experimentation*

When we're starting to explore and getting ourselves organized in step 3, things happening on the physical level tend to include getting diagnostic or further testing, or experimentation.

Sometimes we clear a space for a period of observing ourselves and our physical symptoms or processes. For example, in Susun Weed's book *Menopausal Years: The Wise Woman Way,* she offers a process for healing. Her first step toward resolving any issue is to do nothing, and observe.

We could also be doing something as mundane as creating a repository or file folder for our research and the information we are gathering. For me, that is a powerful way of creating the space for my journey.

■ **Emotional***: Feel and express, relate your feelings to your thoughts*
By the time we get to step 3, we're often coming to grips with difficult emotions from the earlier steps, and are more able to express and release our feelings.

It's also a time that we might be tying our feelings to our thoughts. Sometimes our thoughts are causing certain feelings, and we can learn to think different thoughts in order to generate different feelings. For example, when I doubted whether it was even possible to completely heal my low back pain, that thought was generating a feeling of hopelessness. The decision to change my belief about the possibility of healing in turn generated feelings of hope and empowerment.

Learning to identify where your feelings are coming from

and how to process and release those feelings can be very liberating. It takes your feelings from possessing you to you owning and being in charge of them. As a yoga teacher I studied with once put it: "My feelings are not me, but mine".

- **Mental**: *Research, outreach, synthesizing*
  In the mental dimension, it's a time of researching for new ideas and solutions, and to get a new understanding. I find that I can't necessarily get to a solution until I've clearly identified the problem. Once I've done that, then solutions tend to emerge.

  For example, I had chronic back pain for years without really understanding it. As I determined to heal it, I started observing my pain and what seemed to trigger it. I realized that it would sometimes start in my gut, and sometimes start in my low back. Inflammation in either area would frequently trigger pain in the other. As I read books, worked with yoga teachers and chiropractors, and researched back pain online, I got an increasingly clear picture of what my pain was, and where it was coming from.

  Based on that clearer picture, I learned back exercises for strengthening the back, and I started learning new ways of sitting, standing, sleeping and moving that are more in line with how our ancestors did those things, back when almost nobody suffered from back pain.

  In particular, two posture experts were very helpful to me, Esther Gokhale, author of *Eight Steps to a Pain Free Back*, and Dr. Eric Goodman, originator of Foundation Training.

- **Spiritual**: *Visions, dreams, connections*
At this juncture of exploration and outreach, our spiritual experiences can turn to visions and dreams of an expanding nature. As we begin to see new possibilities, our horizons can open up.

We also can make new connections with communities, and with our spirituality. Opening up seems to attract help in the form of guidance, intuitive "hits" and sensing we are on the right path ... or not, in which case we can course-correct.

I often follow my intuition when researching online. Many years ago, I was doing what then was the equivalent of an online search by browsing titles in the bookstore. I was attracted to a title of *Jung, Synchronicity and Human Destiny* by Ira Progoff, which I bought and read. It was to shape my journey for the next several years. From it I learned of another of Ira Progoff's books, *At A Journal Workshop*, which I worked with for years, attending journaling workshops and learning to use journaling to reach deep into myself and my experiences. In fact, I first heard the story that I recounted in the introduction to this book at a journal workshop.

Another time, I was meditating on my concerns about the environment when the single word "sustainability" came into my awareness. I've spent many years unpacking the meaning of that word in my life, and it was part of what led me to become an organic gardener, which has become a hugely important part of my life.

STEP 4 ~ MAKE CHOICES ABOUT APPROACH, FEELINGS, CHANGES

It's the night that makes the dawning.
It's the depths that make the heights.
It's the roots that make the branches.
It's the darkness that gives birth to Light.

— JOEL HEATHCOTE

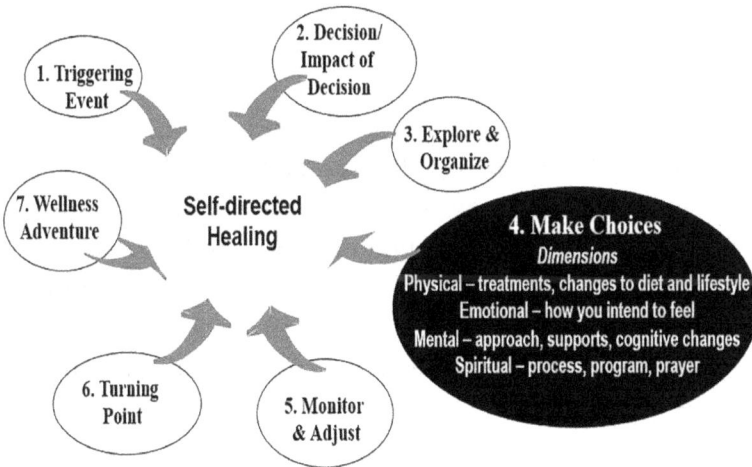

Figure II.5: The model calls out the Make Choices step and the ways it impacts all four dimensions, physical, emotional, mental and spiritual.

In step 4, we may still be exploring and researching, but we begin to make choices about our approach and the changes we need to make. Often we determine we need to claim new or different feelings. For example, people with a cancer diagnosis often find they need to get mad and fight. That emotion can be a conscious choice. I sometimes feel at this point that I need to feel more in touch with my own power and consciously choose to believe in healing.

Others find they need to make changes in their approach. Our RA patient had this to say: "I had to change the way I exercised, and I continue to do different exercise today than what I was doing ten years ago. Thirteen years ago, I was going to the gym, lifting weights, doing cardio. I was doing hard-charging, push, push types of exercise. I started switching to yoga even before the RA was diagnosed. Still, it was a very active yoga practice and fast walking."

Then, one day she went walking on a forest path, and she couldn't finish the path due to excruciating back pain. So now, instead of strenuous high-impact exercise, "I go to my community recreation center and take water exercise. I can run faster than ever in the water. I've always loved the water. When I started doing water exercise, it felt really fun, comfortable ... that was synergistic change to all the other changes I made."

She's learned that "if I fuel myself properly, if I sleep enough, I have enough energy."

On the topic of doctors and choices, she says: "It's really challenging, whether in a metro area or in a smaller town, to find the right doctor for who you are. Sometimes you luck into it. I left a bigger practice I totally hated and went to the doctor that diagnosed some recent issues I was having as due to migraines. Now I'm going back to my primary care physician (the one with the bigger practice) to say to him here's

what happened. I don't want to end up with pain medications. I enter into the process of finding a doctor as if it's
online dating. I interview them. I've never had a doctor not
be caring; they just care in their own way. Sometimes that
way suits me, and sometimes it doesn't."

Another woman said her emotions "shifted when I started
to feel better. I realized there are other ways. I felt empowered. Felt like I'm in control, and can make choices that
make me feel better. I'm my own doctor. We have our own
inner doctor. Like having a supportive network of women. I
learned a lot more from other women than I ever did from a
doctor. What you focus on is what you get back. Believing I
can get better (was important to her)."

The woman who took her whole family along on the journey
reports "we rarely see a doctor. I feel that our immune
systems have improved so much that we barely get sick. If
we do get a cold or something, I usually 'fix-it' with natural
remedies. Also, I feel that bacteria or viral infections don't
really get a hold of us anymore – and if they do, they are not
here to stay. I have not had one sinus infection since [making
healing changes]; my husband's acid reflux has disappeared;
and the kids can turn on and off their stuffed noses by what
they eat ☺"

I want to highlight that last remark about her kids. That they
can turn on and off their symptoms with their food choices.
That is a hugely empowering realization for any of us,
knowing that the power is in our hands. And if, one day, we
don't make all the best choices and we get sick or feel bad, we
know how to turn it around the next day. And we don't even
have to beat ourselves up over it. We know what happened
and it's no big deal.

On a similar note, my doctor of Traditional Chinese Medicine once told me: "You shouldn't drink alcohol. But if you do, eat a pear the next morning to help your liver." That was an empowering recommendation which left the choices up to me.

The Dimensions:

- **Physical**: *Treatments, changes to diet and lifestyle*
  Many of the choices that we make at this step revolve around the physical dimension. We might decide we need to make dietary changes or start taking nutritional supplements, or we might need to add more water into our day.

  This also is the level where we might make certain changes to our lifestyle, deciding to exercise more or change how we exercise to be more compatible with our constitution. In fact, we may have determined in the previous step what our physical type or constitution is, and may have a whole series of recommendations based on our type that we implement in this step.

  For example, I'm a combination of "pitta" and "vata" in the Ayurvedic system of constitutional types. Knowing that has led me to seek out cooling foods when I experience a pitta imbalance, or too much internal heat. If it's my vata energy that's out of balance, I'd be inclined to look for grounding foods to deal with the "spacey" tendencies that vata can summon.

  Another typing system that many people explore and decide to implement at this step is Dr. D'Adamo's blood type system. He recommends dietary changes based on your blood type, on the theory that certain foods have chemistry similar to the different blood types. Just as you wouldn't want a transfusion of type O blood when you're type A, you also wouldn't want to eat a food that mimics the chemistry of type O. That's an over-simplification of the theory, which you can learn more about in his book *Eat Right For Your Type*. Dr. D'Adamo also goes beyond dietary changes to recommend types of exercise and movement, herbs, and teas that are determined by your blood type.

■ **Emotional**: *How you intend to feel*
The emotional dimension of this step, where we're making choices about our approaches, our feelings and our treatments, is all about conscious choice centered on our feelings. At one time, I used to think that feelings just "happened" to me, and there was nothing I could do about it. But I've since learned that we have a lot of choice about how we are going to feel.

For example, I've lately been playing around with feelings of anxiety and nervousness, say before an important meeting or an interview, and turning them into feelings of excitement and positive anticipation. Once you get the hang of it, it may surprise you to see how easy it can be to redirect your feelings toward the way you want to feel.

A tool that comes in handy in this step is visualization. Athletes often visualize their entire performance ahead of time, including how they will feel when they're actually doing it. And research shows that, on a feeling level, there's often no difference between the world we imagine and the physical world we experience. In other words, we react emotionally to both an imagined event, such as an athletic performance, and to the actual event. And we can practice ahead of time to pattern the feelings the way we want them to be.

Another tool on the emotional level is Emotional Freedom Technique (EFT). It's a method that uses tapping on the meridian points to help release feelings, and also to program in changes in our thoughts and feelings. Many people report having greater dominion of their feelings through the use of EFT.

This step can also involve how we feel about the choices we are in the process of making. For many of us, there are emotional attachments to our current choices, in food and in behaviors. It can be a challenge to give up those attachments and adopt healthier choices.

Other feelings you may experience in this step are liberation, empowerment and new resourcefulness.

■ **Mental***: Approach, supports, cognitive changes*
Just as we can choose how we are going to feel about circumstances, we also can decide how we want to think. We can employ positive thinking. And I don't mean denial. The adoption of positive thinking should occur after your feelings have been acknowledged, expressed, and released. Otherwise, the unexpressed feelings will gum up the thinking, and may render it less than positive.

Some people choose at this point to use affirmations to anchor and support their new thoughts. Phrases like the classic "Every day in every way I'm getting better

and better" from French psychologist Emile Coue
can actually make us feel better, and even actually be
better.

Cognitive therapy is another way people choose to
change their thoughts. It is a type of therapy that's
frequently useful for people dealing with depression
and anxiety.

Visualization also can play a role in both choosing an
approach, and selecting the thoughts that support it.
When we are stuck in a negative thought pattern, it
can help to visualize the pattern itself, and see it slowly
melting or breaking up and falling apart. That breaking up can clear the way for new thoughts to form and
take root.

- **Spiritual**: *Process, program, prayer*
  Metaphysics teaches us that we can effect change in
  the outer world by making small shifts in the inner
  world. As the saying goes "small hinges swing big
  doors."

These changes can take the form of changing beliefs,
or processing thoughts and feelings we want to change.
We also can think in terms of programming. We are
programmed in childhood to think, behave and feel in
certain ways. When we take charge of our own lives,
we can choose to change our programming, inserting
new directives that better serve us.

For example, I was taught not to say no when I was a
child. That was convenient for my parents, for various
reasons, but I can't say it served me well as an adult.

So I had to unravel what was behind my reluctance to say no, and create a new program that countered those old feelings, thoughts and prohibitions. Now I sometimes say no just for the hell of it. ☺

STEP 5 ~ MONITOR AND ADJUST

"Recently a young mother asked for advice. What, she wanted to know, was she to do with a 7-year-old who was obstreperous, outspoken, and inconveniently willful? 'Keep her,' I replied. "

– ANNA QUINDLEN

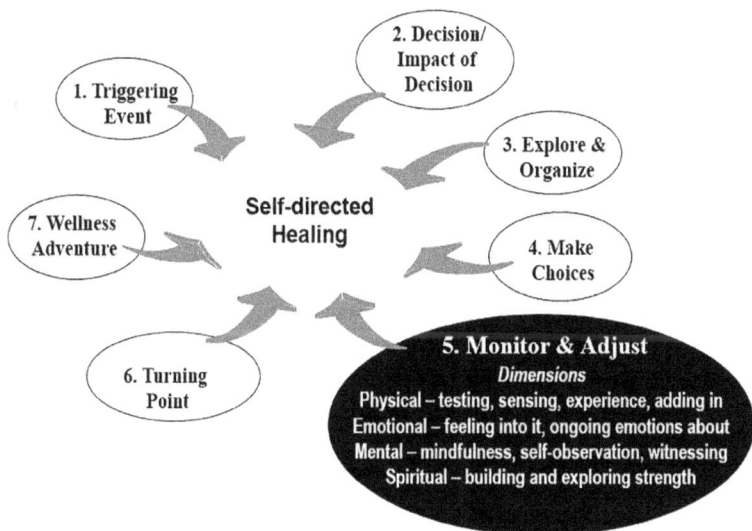

Figure II.6: The model calls out the Monitor & Adjust step and the ways it impacts all four dimensions, physical, emotional, mental and spiritual.

In step five, we often find ourselves building new "muscles," new habits and new strengths. It's here that we gain momentum and return to our former selves, even as we develop new senses of self.

Our RA interviewee reports that she did get the RA under control in about 6 months. She was going to IIN, which played a huge part in her recovery. "Things were going great ... then last fall I started with what I thought was a simple cold, then sinus infections that I could not resolve, and I was also having vertigo on a regular basis. I usually had the vertigo for about 4 hours of a day, then I'd feel woozy and out of sorts for a few days, then I'd have more vertigo. I wasn't able to feel stable as I walked around. So as a massage therapist again, (I was unable to work). When vertigo hits, you have to just lay down and do nothing. It was compounded with rapidly losing my hearing. That started in November. By January, my husband and I were researching disability, discussing whether I'd be able to continue both coaching and massage ... he had to drive me places."

"It turns out the diagnosis – I went to Johns Hopkins hospital in Baltimore – the doctor says, you have migraines causing these symptoms. He said to change my diet. He referred me to a book called Heal Your Headache, by David Buchholz, that details what changes to make. I went on a migraine trigger elimination diet, giving up many of my favorite foods. It was depressing. It was scary and depressing being that sick."

But then she goes on to say "I went to the doctor on Friday, changed my diet on Saturday, and by Tuesday morning, I woke up at 4 am. I could breathe better than I ever had, and I woke up with perfect hearing for 4 hours. I knew within 3 days of starting the diet that I was on the right track; even though it took 2-3 weeks for my hearing to come back completely."

In my own experience, this step carries a strong sense of

observing myself and making changes in a mindful way. I find it's about testing changes or treatments, sensing the effects, and adjusting accordingly. Adding in new approaches for a cumulative effect is also a powerful part of monitoring and adjusting.

Another woman says: "It's ongoing. There's a big tie-in with stress. (I needed to learn) how to relax. I've always been type A, busy, busy. Now I'm trying to define free time for my body to rest, and my mind to rest. One thing that's really helped me is charting my natural cycles ... it's given me tons of insight. (It's helped me to realize) I can do it on my own. There's stuff I can do without having to see a doctor."

Our family-changing woman comments: "I think that our emotions were pretty positive all along the way. I was already a yoga instructor by the time I decided to sign-up for IIN and make dietary changes. Therefore, I'd done a lot of work with my mind already."

"For me personally and also my family it is definitely an ongoing process. I mean, we always gain new knowledge, and that's why for us it would not circle back. But I can also see that there are always challenges along the road and there-fore, the progress is a journey."

The Dimensions:
- **Physical**: *Testing, sensing, experience, adding in*
  Strength can be a physical attribute as well as a mental, emotional and spiritual one. And it often grows in this monitor-and-adjust step, as we get firmly rooted in new ways, new discoveries and new solutions.

In this step, there is often more testing, attention to sensing our bodies and their reactions to the changes we've been making, and how they affect our experience. As we're often past the first round of changes, we can make more changes, adding in the new and allowing the old to fall away.

For example, I'm always adding in nuances in my posture-based program for back pain relief. Every day I make scores of small adjustments in how I stand, sit, and move, adjusting the turnout of a foot, rolling a shoulder back or lengthening my spine in some small way. Changes that I learned by studying the Gokhale Method, by Esther Gokhale, author of *8 Steps to a Pain-Free Back: Natural Posture Solutions for Pain in the Back, Neck, Shoulder, Hip, Knee, and Foot.*

All these little corrections add up over time and can bring about big changes.

For me, they are reducing my back pain to unprecedented lows, and the changes are subtle but effective.

■ **Emotional***: Feeling into it, ongoing emotions about change*
Just as we can monitor and adjust the physical aspects of our health, we can be mindful of our feelings, going into them at times, and tending to our ongoing emotions about our healing.

While it's not helpful to get stuck in our feelings, allowing them some space and letting ourselves be aware of feelings is a good thing.

If I find myself feeling negative, I can make small adjustments, just as I do with my posture. And again, those small changes can add up to big mood shifts toward the positive.

We can also alter our moods with the dietary choices we make, as the chemistry of foods has powerful impacts on mood. If you've ever watched a roomful of kids after they've eaten sugary treats, you know about the food-mood connection.

■ **Mental**: *Mindfulness, self-observation, witnessing*
Mindfulness is a practice that allows us to slow down and really go into a thought or a feeling. Health-care practitioners often notice that their most successful patients have some kind of mindfulness or spiritual practice in their repertoire.

We also, in this step, may be observing ourselves, noticing the nature of our thoughts and how they impact our feelings.

It's a good time for the practice of witnessing, that neutral observation and playing back of what's there without editorializing. Sometimes others can witness for us. Sometimes we can be very moved by witnessing the journeys of others. That's been a part of my experience in writing this book and conducting interviews with people who've taken charge of their own healing. It's been my privilege to witness their stories.

■ **Spiritual**: *Building and exploring strength*
We also find ourselves building new strengths, and exploring how far we've come and how far we can go in

the process of monitoring and making course corrections. If we've made it this far on our journey, we begin
to understand that the same power that brought us
this far will take us the rest of the way. And we begin to
trust that power and know that it is there for us.

When I attended IIN, the social aspects were daunting
at first. But I knew I was building exactly the emotional
muscles I needed for reaching out to others and con-
necting. And as I went along, I became more confident
that those muscles would always be there for me when
I needed them. Indeed, that confidence has revolution-
ized my ability to build relationships.

STEP 6 ~ THE TURNING POINT

"The personal life deeply lived always expands into truths beyond itself."

– ANAIS NIN

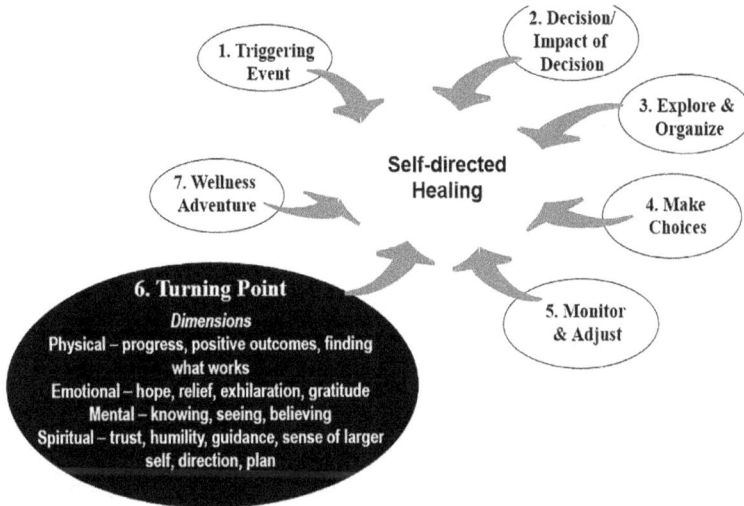

Figure II.7: The model calls out the Turning Point and the ways it impacts all four dimensions, physical, emotional, mental and spiritual.

In step six, we often experience a turning point, where the emotions go from mostly negative to mostly positive. In my experience, it's when I start to get some traction, seeing that the choices I make can make me feel better or worse. It's the point where I start to feel empowered in my health decisions.

And at this point, I have an inner knowing that I'm going to succeed. (By the way, it doesn't have to take a long time to get to this point, and sometimes, you start with this step. Remember, you can start anywhere on this road map.)

One woman I talked to puts it this way: "When I started working with my life coach, he'd often start the call with asking 'what is good in your life today? Or name 3 things you're grateful for ...' to which I'd answer: 'nothing'. During that period of grief he helped with a mindset shift. He was able to take me from that dark place to a place of gratitude in the (space of one phone call)."

Another says she started writing, blogging, and sharing her experience.

"I struggled with over-achieving, stemming from an 'I'm not worth it' attitude. I was eating poorly, and using alcohol and drugs. Then I came to an awareness that I'm worth giving myself the very best. I hope to inspire other women. Things can get pretty dark."

She says her experiences "put her on a path of, if not Catholic, then who are you? I found I was more (interested in) eastern religions, (adopting) Buddhism. Those practices helped me find inner peace. Surrendering, definitely mindfulness and going within. While that whole process (of her illness) was stressful, it was a good thing that happened."

Our RA patient says: "Anytime [you are] dealing with illness, there's a corner that you turn. When you start to remember how it felt before all that started. On the migraines I can tell you exactly where that point was, what changed was – this is a struggle – turn the corner and it's like the light at the end of the tunnel is really a light, not an oncoming train. Now I know I can trust myself, and that my decisions make long-term sense. That morning where I could hear perfectly, I was idiotic giddy, stupid happy. Also really frustrated to think I had that fabulous four hours, and then four hours later, I was back in the quicksand ..."

"Before a turning point, when feeling so ill and compromised, I feel fragile – like every little gust of wind is going to send me over the cliff. Not having control, just never knowing what's going to be the next difficult situation. For me when I turn the corner, I feel strong again, feel like myself again, the essence of who I am. I can trust my body ... That sense of confidence is what we lose when in pain and ill. You find that turning point and little by little you test the waters and figure out how much you can swim, then you find you have your confidence back. Okay that little thing I used to do, I'm going to try, and then there's that fabulous exaltation of oh my god, I did it... I did it."

The Dimensions:

■ **Physical**: *Progress, positive outcomes, finding what works*

The turning point is often the step where we recognize undeniable progress and positive outcomes. Our pain diminishes, or our symptoms recede. Maybe the nodules or lumps found on an earlier CAT scan show up smaller or disappear on a new one.

It's the point where we see that all the changes are working for us, and we're learning how to identify other things we can do to improve.

For example, when my lower back pain was at its

worst, I was experiencing pain daily, it woke me up at night and kept me awake, and my balance issues sometimes made walking difficult. The backs of my legs were constantly in knots and my feet got numb if I walked for more than 10 minutes.

My turning point came when I found an exercise, just one move, that would stretch out my glutes when they'd been in spasm for months if not years. I learned this move, called the "Founder," from the work of Dr. Eric Goodman and his Foundation Training.

This one maneuver stretched the muscles out enough that the night after I learned it, I felt some bone pop back into place underneath my glutes, and I slept through the night. That was when I knew I was onto something.

■ **Emotional**: *Hope, relief, exhilaration, gratitude*
The emotions that show up at this step tend to be in the positive range. From hope to relief that you've found something that works, to the exhilaration of regaining your former physical power.

Sometimes giddy with relief, we see the light at the end of the tunnel, and we know we're going to be okay. This is often the place where gratitude wells up and we appreciate all the help we've received.

My feelings about the turning point with my low back pain included all of the above and a sense of confidence as well. Confidence in my body, confidence in my healing process, and confidence in the power that fuels the healing.

■ **Mental**: *Knowing, seeing, believing*
Believing often, maybe always, precedes seeing, even though we've been taught that it's the opposite – "seeing is believing". The power of our minds – that mind over matter – is evident at the turning point, as the beliefs we've changed take hold and our reality changes accordingly.

In our mind's eye, what we see can be just the harbinger of things to come, and we can choose our future, and allow ourselves to pull in the future we choose through the choices we make today.

When I say mind, I'm talking not about the brain, which certainly is a marvelous instrument, but the "I" that inhabits the brain. The non-local entity that is the self, and is the owner of the body ... the occupant.

■ **Spiritual**: *Trust, humility, guidance, sense of larger self, direction, plan*
At the turning point, we often experience new levels of trust, in ourselves and in our higher selves, or inner guidance. We may have keener sense of a Self larger than us, who is behind and holding together the direction we take.

If you've ever practiced meditation, mindfulness or participated in psychotherapy you may have felt this invisible force that works beyond the limits of the conscious mind and steers us through challenging times. You can see it in the way that when you're ready to face some issue, it suddenly starts appearing everywhere. Like when you decide to buy a new Camry and suddenly you see Camry's everywhere you look.

We also may find ourselves taking a new direction at this step, knowing we've started down a new path, trusting its wisdom without necessarily knowing where we'll end up.

STEP 7 ~ A WELLNESS ADVENTURE

Throw your dreams into space like a kite, and you do not know what it will bring back, a new life, a new friend, a new love, a new country.

– ANAIS NIN

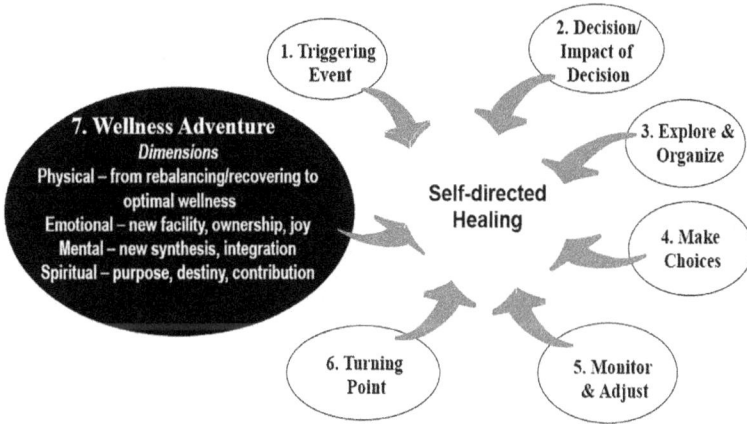

Figure II.8: The model calls out the Wellness Adventure and the ways it impacts all four dimensions, physical, emotional, mental and spiritual.

The last step is what I like to call the Wellness Adventure stage. It's when the journey has turned into an exciting adventure and all the changes we've made, the help we've found, and the choices and decisions become something greater. This stage is characterized by feelings of gratitude, a desire to give back, and the sense of connection to something greater than us.

It's also about going beyond "just" getting back into balance. When I said to my chiropractor that I'd gotten out of balance, he wanted to know if I meant it the way he would, as a misalignment, or some other way. I think it's more my Chinese doctor's definition: When you get sick it means you've become out of balance.

When you get seriously out of balance as I did a couple of years ago with my back pain, it's also an opportunity to go beyond just eliminating symptoms. Actually it's an opening – it's a message. I can take it as a key, and if I employ it properly I can connect to the power of synergy, creating exponential improvement.

If I listen to the message, the whispers, I can go beyond just eliminating symptoms. Maybe by addressing this, I can go for more health than just rebalancing, just returning to homeostasis. When a natural system evolves it moves to a higher level of organization. It crystallizes a new level of intelligence.

Your system can get out of balance due to anything from bad behaviors – food, drink, too much caffeine, sugar, drugs – to trying to live with too much stress, which unfortunately is a very common way people get out of balance. When it happens, you can learn to regard it as an opportunity for growth. That's one aspect of this idea of the wellness adventure.

I can assume that I can make an adventure of my challenges. And in doing so, the messages I receive can become the guide to my life's journey, my Soul's journey. Indeed that may be their highest function.

And it doesn't mean you have to be perfect, or have perfect health. One person I spoke with said: "I really believe that this kind of stuff I'm dealing with is my version of a marathon. I didn't know that when the race started, but never tell me I'm not running the race of my life. It is my life, and it is a marathon. Every time I think I've made it to the finish line, something else comes up ..."

Another person says that wellness adventure is "a good term for it. The whole thing gets this spunky energy around it of how can I learn more."

One interviewee reports that "even figuring out what to eat is an adventure." She has also experimented with a lot of alternatives, colonics, acupuncture, and so forth.

She confirms that "I see this as an ongoing journey. No end to it because we are ever-evolving. our environment changes and so do we, we adapt and adjust with it. So yes, definitely a wellness adventure."

The Dimensions:
- ■ **Physical**: *From rebalancing-recovering to optimal wellness*
  The wellness adventure step is obviously an ongoing journey in our lives. It's often the place where people report going from getting back in balance to having their health take off in new positive directions. Whether it's making the leap from student to teacher as a holistic health coach or yoga instructor, or some other new direction they hadn't previously considered.

  This is the place where Olympic and professional athletes tend to hang out, always looking to optimize their performance. Not that they don't have health issues like the rest of us, as many do deal with lots of malfunction and pain. But when they get it right, they're into the wellness adventuring territory.

For me, going to IIN and being in the Immersion Program were wellness adventures where I learned from some of the leading lights in holistic wellness. What fun!

Some people also take wellness adventuring literally and make it a part of their adventure travel. David (Avocado) Wolfe comes to mind as someone who travels the globe looking for new (and ancient) health solutions, foods and super foods.

■ **Emotional**: *New facility, ownership, joy*
True to its name, the wellness adventure can bring joy and fun to our lives. My friend Janet goes on adventures around the world, some of which offer healing, such as the time she met a Shaman in Ecuador; all of which bring her joy.

We may find that our emotions are easier to handle and we have a new facility with our feelings in many different situations. Relationships may come easier, as we feel happier, lighter and more confident. And we learn to own our feelings in ways that are easy for others to honor. When I'm comfortable with and know that my feelings are okay, it's always easier for others to hear them as well.

■ **Mental**: *New synthesis, integration*
It's in this step that we often notice a new integration

in our thinking. As in the extreme case of The Three Faces of Eve and other multiple personality disorders, a new identity can emerge which helps to integrate the rest of the personalities.

In a less extreme way, we can find we have more space for, and acceptance of, all the different sides of ourselves.

Sometimes we find that we have a new synthesis from all the exploring and experiences we've had along the way. A new way of combining things, ideas and information, that creates a new sense of ease.

■ **Spiritual**: *Purpose, destiny, contribution*
In the wellness adventure step, people often report having a new sense of purpose, a desire to give back and to make a contribution to society. They tie themselves to a sense of destiny, and feel that their life's work becomes clear.

Having learned to turn challenges into adventures, we feel more confident than ever in our own faculties. We often take on challenges that just a few years before would have seemed unthinkable.Knowing that we have help and support, we can step further out of our comfort zone, trusting ourselves in novel and interesting ways. We find we can give voice to our desires, or that situations that used to frighten us now delight.

It's an Iterative Process
The thing to understand is that it's an iterative process. We don't proceed on a straight line through this process only once. We move in and out of it. We sometimes take one step

forward and two steps back. But then we can make a choice to just start moving forward again.

One influence that shaped my ideas over the years was a book called *Composing a Life*, a collection of the life stories of five women, examined from an anthropologist's perspective. The author, Mary Catherine Bateson, the daughter of anthropologist Gregory Bateson and Margaret Mead, the author of *Coming of Age in Samoa*, traces the uniquely feminine style of weaving a life. It is a style that is made up of advances mixed with setbacks. In creative endeavors, particularly in the lives of women, she asserts, we learn that sometimes the best progress does not occur in linear fashion.

In the male-oriented world of singular focus, creating with a capital "C," projects are conceived, they are capitalized, and they proceed from start to finish without interruption. The resources assigned to the project are protected from intrusions, and the simplest, most direct path is followed to bring the project to a conclusion. In a way, this single-focus style is seductive; in a way it's intuitively obvious – how else can we get anything done?

But in the realities of day-to-day experience, we often go without this luxury of singular focus, and often it serves us better than we know. In *Composing a Life*, Mary Catherine Bateson articulates the understanding that sometimes the way is unclear; that sometimes we must fall back and regroup and rethink. Sometimes the way is blocked and we haven't the wherewithal to unblock it ourselves. We must wait. It is foreign to the impatient mind of today's America, this concept of biding our time.

Yet it is an idea that can be useful in the larger scheme of things, and in our understanding of the healing journey. For this idea better describes the reality of healing and of personal growth. It's an imperfect process, and one that meanders more than it drives directly to the place we think we want to go.

PART III

~

APPLYING THE SIMPLE METHOD

This section discusses how to apply the seven-step process for taking charge of your own health. It covers the interview process and its results, and it includes profiles of the interviewees whose journeys were most representative of the simple method.

Applying the Process

First, try to determine where you are relative to the process road map. It may be obvious to you, or it may take some thought. Often it's more obvious to a beginner than to someone who's been on a healing journey for a while.

If you're not sure, test it. Pick a step and assume that's where you are. Now see if it fits. Are your feelings similar to the ones described in the process steps? Do you relate to the stories you're reading? If so, you're in the right place. If not, maybe take a look at the step before or the step after and see if it makes more sense to you.

There's no one right way, and no perfect answer. The idea is to let the process guide you on all the dimensions involved. And sometimes to see if you can rise to the positive experiences you're reading about.

The interviews and their results
The interviews, along with my own experience, serve to illustrate how people experience this journey.

The interviews that I conducted while writing this book were based on the questions below, including the explanation that I used as preface. You can see from the questions that I didn't start the interviews from a blank slate, asking open-ended questions and tallying the results. Instead, my intention was to start with a model distilled from my own experience and observations of my healing journey, and see if the people I interviewed validated that model and in what ways their journeys differed from mine and from each other's.

The Preface

I believe that healing occurs on many levels, and I'm calling out 4 dimensions in the book:

1 **Physical**
2 **Emotional**
3 **Mental**
4 **Spiritual**

So I'm interested in exploring each of these at every step of the journey, and how they fit.

I'm particularly interested in the emotional aspects because I think they can make it challenging to make health decisions on your own, or against the dictates of authorities.

Please feel free to pay more attention to the questions that interest you below, and don't feel that you have to answer them all. Also, feel free to start with just telling your story in your own words.

The Questions

1 *How did you get started on your healing journey - did something happen? An event, a diagnosis, etc.?*

2 *How did that feel?*

3 *What made you want to take charge of your own health? Was it an active "I'm taking charge - out of my way!", or was it more gradual or a result of necessity (i.e. medical science had little to offer)?*

4 *What happened next after you decided to take charge? Were there shifts in your physical symptoms, feelings, thoughts or spiritual process?*

5 *How did family and friends react to your decision?*

6 *What kinds of supports did you find for your process?*

7 *What happened next?*

8 *Do you see your healing process as ongoing and circling back to previous steps at times (i.e. an iterative process)? In what way?*

9 *Have you learned to follow your own approach for multiple ailments?*

10 *Tell me about your experiences with doctors. Good? Bad? Indifferent?*

11 *Have you ever felt threatened or bullied by a doctor, nurse or practitioner? If so, what was that about?*

12 *Was there a turning point where the emotions went from negative to positive?*

13 *If so, what happened after that turning point?*

14 *Did you ever find that the diet or lifestyle changes, treatments and approaches you found acted synergistically? (i.e. whole more than the sum of the parts - or like you got a cumulative effect?)*

15 *Was there ever a point where you felt that rather than being in a frightening, compromised position, you were on a "wellness adventure"? If so, how did that happen?*

16 *Is there anything you'd like to add that I didn't ask about?*

17 *Is there anyone else you know that I should interview? If so, can you please provide a referral?*

The results of the interviews were amazing. The experiences of these strong, powerful women that I interviewed went beyond validation of my ideas to validate my experiences and my feelings. They gave me the courage to tell my own story, even as I admired their courage in telling their stories.

In fact, I'd go so far as to say the experience of interviewing these women was healing for me. There was something beautiful in witnessing their journeys, and that beauty was healing in itself.

In the following chapters, we'll explore the results of the interviews, and profile the women whose journeys best exemplify the steps of the self-directed healing journey.

The following profiles are intended to show how each woman's journey looked, as she passed through each of the 7 steps of the process.

Profile 1

~

Our Patient with Rheumatoid Arthritis

The Persona
Massage therapist, with diagnosis of rheumatoid arthritis.

Illnesses and Challenges
- Rheumatoid arthritis
- Migraines
- Debilitating vertigo
- Loss of hearing

Healing Ways
- Dietary changes
- Migraine elimination diet
- Changes to exercise

Healing Results
- Arthritis mitigated, able to function and work as massage therapist
- Hearing fully restored
- Vertigo cleared

Where she is today
- Actively working as a massage therapist and pain relief coach.
- Confident in her ability to heal herself

THE TRIPTYCH — HOW SHE
NAVIGATED HER JOURNEY

Step 1 – The Triggering event

"Before there was a diagnosis, there was a big shift in my comfort level with my own life. I was 37 years old, had been working in the stressful world of sales and marketing for 17? years. Right after 911 happened, I starting asking what kind of difference I'm making in the world. I decided to become a massage therapist (a decision that was a whole journey in itself). I wanted to have more of a one-on-one connection with people. So I went from sitting in a chair, not using my body much, to depending on my body to work in order to make a living.

"I started to understand, even though I was always active, that I really needed to kick it up to another level with my exercise. I built the massage practice to a full-time business. About six years in, I started to have tension in my hands, along with swelling and it was very uncomfortable and scary. I'm grateful to say that I got pretty quickly to a diagnosis – it only took two to three months to get to a diagnosis of rheumatoid arthritis. That part was pretty painless for me. I also had tremendous fatigue. My hands and knees hurt. I had lots of little pain spots. But there was also this crushing fatigue. I was 43 years old."

When I asked about the emotional side of her diagnosis, she told me: "I felt like I had to embark on this whole new educational endeavor. I felt very burdened by having to learn everything. Usually I'm learning because I want to and I'm excited about it, but this time I had to. It was frustrating to be forced into that. It was scary because I see from my mother's experience with RA, if I don't get this under control, I see what can happen. It's pretty terrifying."

Step 2 - Decision-Impact of Decision

"For me, feeling sick is an incredible loss of control. That sets you off your center. Even just making small changes and starting to figure stuff out, makes me feel like okay, okay, the disease isn't in control, the doctors aren't in control. It's up to me and my body."

Step 3 - Explore & Organize

"A couple of people had come into my life fairly close to my RA diagnosis that also have RA. That was more like, it was nice to have someone to call and talk to about stuff. One of them gave me the referral to the rheumatologist. I also got involved in quite a supportive online community where I used Twitter to connect to a bunch of people that were really strangers to me. At that point I was on Twitter all the time, which made a huge difference."

Step 4 - Make Choices about Approach, Feelings, Changes

"I had to change the way I exercised, and I continue to do different exercises today than what I was doing ten years ago. Thirteen years ago, I was going to the gym, lifting weights, doing cardio. I was doing hard-charging, push, push types of exercise. I started switching to yoga even before the RA was diagnosed. Still, it was a very active yoga practice and fast walking."

Then, when she went walking on a forest path, she couldn't finish the path due to excruciating back pain. So now, instead of strenuous high-impact exercise, "I go to my community recreation center and take water exercise. I can run faster than ever in the water. I've always loved the water. When I started doing water exercise, it felt really fun, comfortable... that was synergistic change to all the other changes I made."

She's learned that "if I fuel myself properly, if I sleep enough, I have enough energy."

On the topic of doctors and choices, she says: "It's really challenging, whether in a metro area or in a smaller town, to find the right doctor for who you are. Sometimes you luck into it. I left a bigger practice I totally hated and went to the doctor that diagnosed some recent issues I was having as due to migraines. Now I'm going back to my primary care physician (the one with the bigger practice) to say to him: here's what happened. I don't want to end up with pain meds. I enter into the process of finding a doctor as if it's online dating. I interview them. I've never had a doctor not be caring; they just care in their own way. Sometimes that way suits me, and sometimes it doesn't."

Step 5 - Monitor and Adjust

When her doctor told her she had migraines, "he said to change my diet. He referred me to a book on what changes to make. I went on a migraine trigger elimination diet, giving up many of my favorite foods. It was depressing. It was scary and depressing being that sick."

But then she goes on to say: "I went to the doctor on Friday, changed my diet on Saturday, and by Tuesday morning, I woke up at 4 am. I could breathe better than I ever had, and I woke up with perfect hearing for 4 hours. I knew within 3 days of starting that I was on the right track; even though it took 2-3 weeks for my hearing to come back completely."

Step 6 - The Turning Point

"Anytime [you are] dealing with illness, there's a corner that you turn. When you start to remember how it felt before all that started. On the migraines I can tell you exactly where that point was, what changed was – this is a struggle – turn the corner and it's like the light at the end of the tunnel is really a light, not an oncoming train. Now I know I can trust myself, and that my decisions make long-term sense. That morning where I could hear perfectly, I was idiotic giddy, stupid happy. Also really frustrated to think I had that fabulous four hours, and then four hours later, back in the quicksand ..."

"Before a turning point, when feeling so ill and compromised, I feel fragile – like every little gust of wind is going to send me over the cliff. Not having control, just never knowing what's going to be the next difficult situation. For me, when I turn the corner, I feel strong again, feel like myself again, the essence of who I am. I can trust my body ... That sense of confidence is what we lose when in pain and ill. You find that turning point and little by little you test the waters and figure out how much you can swim, then you find you have your confidence back. Okay, that little thing I used to do, I'm going to try, and then there's that fabulous exaltation of oh my god, I did it... I did it."

Step 7 - A Wellness Adventure

"I really believe that this kind of stuff I'm dealing with is my version of a marathon. I didn't know that when the race started, but never tell me I'm not running the race of my life. It is my life, and it is a marathon. Every time I think I've made it to the finish line, something else comes up..."

PROFILE 2

~

THE REGISTERED NURSE

The Persona
Registered nurse and health coach

Illnesses and Challenges
- Healing care for her hospital patients
- PMS
- Knee problems

Healing Ways
- Dietary changes for herself and her patients and friends
- Reiki
- Healing herbs and foods

Healing Results
- Patients better served
- Knees "buzzing with energy" and healed
- Greatly improved energy from dietary changes

Where she is today
- When friends run into health issues, her family tells them to call her
- Thriving Reiki practice
- Published author

THE TRIPTYCH — HOW SHE NAVIGATED HER JOURNEY

Step 1 - The Triggering event

Her "very first patient had suffered his second or third heart attack, and I knew what I was doing was not going to be healing, like the food I was required to feed him, with pats of margarine on instant mashed potatoes, pressed chicken, and canned gravy. It was disgusting! At that time in hospitals, it was still common to take patients outside to smoke a cigarette, and I took him out to smoke, removed his oxygen so he could smoke, then put it back." Soon after that she started learning about healing with herbs and food.

She reported feeling "anger at them feeding us this line, and frustration with the system, knowing it wasn't healing but not knowing where to go from there." But once she let those feelings go, she started meeting people in all kinds of healing arts, started eating better herself and found it "amazing how you feel great. As my contacts evolved, making connections with people who "get" healing, they're just deep people who have a connection with spirituality, and you feed off of that. It's a learning journey, and you want that energy that these people have."

Step 2 – Decision and Impact of Decision

She started eating better, and found it amazing how you feel great.

"As my contacts evolved, the connection with people who get healing, they're just deep people who have a connection with spirituality, you feed off that. It's a learning journey, you want that energy. "

Step 3 - Explore & Organize

She found "healing people. When you open your door to that energy, people find you, sometimes in the strangest places. I had no idea what Reiki was (an energy healing practice), but a teacher I worked with introduced me to his mother, saying she does this voodoo thing, I think it will help your knees. She (the mother) did a treatment on me. The energy buzzing through my body was crazy. I had to find out what this was and how to do it for other people."

Step 4 - Make Choices about approach, feelings, changes

"I always tell clients, when we first start (to work together), to heal your problem you need to heal emotionally and spiritually. I tell them we'll start with physical and whole foods. Once they realize I know, and can be helpful, I always recommend something such as yoga or tai chi".

Step 5 - Monitor and Adjust

"I have found that my daily yoga helps with this [step]. Yoga has created a space in my life where I can observe myself, without criticism. I pay attention to how my lifestyle choices and behaviors affect how I feel and move through my day interacting with myself and others. When I know a particular behavior is not serving my highest good, I can much more easily remove it and replace it with something that does serve my higher good and healing myself."

Step 6 - The Turning Point

"Yoga helps me to get to this point so much more quickly now. Sometimes I am even instantaneously here."

"When we create mindfulness through a regular yoga practice (or any other form of body awareness exercises: Tai

Chi, Qi Gong, Tae Kwon Do), we consciously make healthier choices in all areas of our lives. When we stop the constant chatter inside our heads and still our minds through mindfulness activities (yoga and other body awareness exercises), we tend to make choices that are in alignment with what is best for our health without feeling deprived. This is because we have learned to live in the present moment and are aligned in body, mind and spirit. That is the awareness that Yoga brings to our being."

Step 7 - A Wellness Adventure

Says that wellness adventure is "a good term for it. The whole thing gets this spunky energy around it of how can I learn more."

PROFILE 3

~

THE MOM

The Persona
Mom, Holistic health practitioner, yoga instructor

Illnesses and Challenges
- Husband had huge problems with Acid Reflux (took Tums as if it was candy)
- Mom had problems with sinus infections, recurring about 3-4 times a year.
- Our kids were always "stuffed" and the youngest had ear infections, one after another.

Healing Ways
- Dietary changes for herself and her family
- Dairy free
- Yoga

Healing Results
- Our immune systems have improved so much that we barely get sick
- Bacteria or viral infections don't really get a hold of us anymore (and if they do, they are not here to stay)
- Has not had one sinus infection since making these changes
- Husband's acid reflux has disappeared
- Kids turn on/off their stuffed noses by what they eat ☺

Where she is today
- Board-certified holistic health practitioner, AADP
- Certified yoga instructor, RYT & Reiki practitioner
- Certified resiliency trainer
- Certified personal trainer, AAFA

THE TRIPTYCH — HOW SHE NAVIGATED HER JOURNEY

Step 1 - The Triggering event

"I was always interested in natural remedies and alternative approaches to health, however, never thought about food as one of those remedies. Then I had a friend who lived the "organic life" and she taught me more and told me about it; gave me more information on the topic. She was also the one who told me about IIN. We ended up in the same class together."

Step 2 - Decision-Impact of Decision

"I grew up in Germany and was accustomed to herbs and alternative sources of medicine (homeopathy, for example). Therefore, I was open to the idea [of taking charge of our health with natural approaches]."

"I never liked to see the doctors too much. However, I never knew that food could have such a big impact. A friend of mine wanted to sign up for IIN and told me about it. I looked into it and thought – wow, that's it. That's what I want to do. I learned with IIN and gradually changed our diets, which completely took care of all the health issues we had in the house. I used to suffer from chronic sinusitis... it's all gone.I just felt it was right for me and my family.

"However, I/we did run in some what I'd call 'social problems.' Friends and even German family of mine would make fun of our new eating habits. They'd joke about all the greens we'd eat and call me Hippie. I just decided that I didn't care... and we kept on our path."

Step 3 - Explore & Organize

"Initial changes were not always easy. For example, I am from Germany. We eat a lot of cold cuts and meat. Well, when we decided as a family to not eat cold cuts anymore, the change was huge. (It was) the same with dairy. Now we are dairy free, but it is a constant journey."

"My husband had huge problems with acid reflux (took Tums as if it was candy). I had problems with sinus infections, recurring about 3-4 times a year. Our kids were always "stuffed" and the youngest had ear infections, one after another. After we made the dietary changes, things changed and we began to see a difference. So, it was a gradual change for us - one step at a time, but you could witness the results."

"At first, I was pretty defensive. My IIN health coach told me in our first session that I needed to get off milk and any types of animal products. It was just too big of a step for me to take at once - and I am not sure if I will ever be vegan again.

We ended up trying it as a family for 6-7 months and included Gluten-free as well. By now, I can see changes in my energy level as soon as I eat, for the better or worse. Our bodies are sensitized ..."

"My husband was the driving force at times and the kids just had to follow along. For the most part they were really good about not being picky with the food change. Small steps at a time..."

Step 4 - Make Choices about Approach, Feelings, Changes

"We rarely see a doctor. I feel that our immune system has improved so much that we barely get sick. If we do get a cold or something, I usually "fix-it" with natural remedies. Also, I feel that bacteria or viral infections don't really get a hold of us anymore - and if they do, they are not here to stay. I have not had one sinus infection since; my husband's acid reflux has disappeared and the kids can turn on and off their stuffed noses by what they eat ;-)"

Step 5 - Monitor and Adjust
"For me personally, and also my family, it is definitely an ongoing process. I mean, we always gain new knowledge and that's why for us it would not circle back. But I can also see that there are always challenges along the road and therefore, the progress is a journey."

Step 6 - The Turning Point
"I think that our emotions were pretty positive all along the way. I was already a yoga instructor by the time I decided to sign-up for IIN and make dietary changes. Therefore, did a lot of work with my mind already.

Step 7 - A Wellness Adventure
"I see this as an ongoing journey. No end to it because we are ever-evolving. Our environment changes and so do we; we adapt and adjust with it. So yes, definitely a wellness adventure."

CONCLUSION

Dreams pass into the reality of action. From the actions stems the dream again; and this interdependence produces the highest form of living.

– ANAIS NIN

In this book, I've attempted to provide a road map, the seven-step process showing a simple method that anyone can use to learn to take charge of their own health.

I sincerely believe that if you follow the simple process, are open to help in its many forms and stay with the process through the challenges it will present, you can change your life and heal yourself. I know I've done that many times over by engaging in the process detailed in this book.

In the last few chapters of this book, we've seen how I and the women interviewed for the book experienced our own healing journeys, and we've encountered variations on the themes that are depicted by the seven-step process. Some people experience the dimensions in each step differently, but overall their stories bear out the progression through these seven stages of healing.

The stories of women who've taken charge of their own healing have illustrated each step or aspect of the method, and how it feels, how it works, and what it means.

In my own journey, I see this recurring phenomenon: Some of the most powerful healers are the people who have healed their own illnesses, by going out on their own, doing the research, going deeply into the messages of their disease, and allowing those messages to lead them into their life journey.

It's my hope that anyone who has received a threatening diagnosis will find this book both helpful and supportive in deciding "where do I go from here?"

It's my hope that people who want to prevent or reverse chronic disease will find in this handbook an example of how they might approach and think about their health in ways that empower.

It's my hope that people who are already healthy, but want to take their health to the next level or optimize their performance will find the methods in this book give them the sense of what a wellness adventure can be and can do for your total health.

In conclusion, if you ever wanted to be more in charge of your health and your life, this book is intended for you.

Appendix and Resources

Template for Action Plan

Instructions: Fill out as you receive recommendations from a practitioner or based on results of research or other information you have gathered. You'll gather information over time and this action plan provides a place to organize and act on the information. When something works, keep doing it and make it a part of your regular regimen. When it doesn't, try something else.

A space is provided for recording how the actions made you feel and the results you saw. You can record goals and results separately in a log or journal, or you can fill out a new copy of the template every 2 weeks.)

Date:

Goals (List two or three actions from the categories below to be adopted over next two weeks):

```
┌─────────────────────────────────────────┐
│                                         │
│                                         │
│                                         │
└─────────────────────────────────────────┘
```

Results (Record your experiences and results here):

```
┌─────────────────────────────────────────┐
│                                         │
│                                         │
│                                         │
└─────────────────────────────────────────┘
```

Nutritional supplements (List any vitamins or supplements you have identified)

```
[                                        ]
```

Dietary changes (List any specific changes to your diet, e.g. foods to eliminate or to add)

```
[                                        ]
```

Super foods (List any super foods you have identified)

```
[                                        ]
```

Herbs and herbal teas (List any herbs and herbal teas you have identified)

```
[                                        ]
```

Exercise and movement (List activities such as Qi Gong, Yoga, back strengthening exercises, posture improvements, swimming, stretching and walking)

```
[                                        ]
```

Practitioners (List providers such as chiropractor, massage therapist, acupuncturist, doctor, and osteopath)

```
```

Techniques (List any techniques you have identified, such as Emotional Freedom Technique, energy healing, and Reiki)

```
```

Rituals (List any rituals you have identified)

```
```

Other supports (List supports such as a support group, an informative online community, an accountability partner, a holistic health coach)

```
```

Sample Action Plan

Action Plan: This sample addresses Migraine Trigger Syndrome, but your the action plan should be customized to your unique experience and needs.
The sample below can serve as a starting point, but it's not comprehensive to everything you could do. A friend of mine who has migraines has found a bracelet specifically designed for migraines that she swears by, and another friend emphasizes the importance of getting enough sleep in reducing migraine triggers. Your plan should be informed by your own research and experience.

Date: 09/07/2014

Goals (List two or three actions from the categories below to be adopted over next two weeks):

---

1. Eliminate or reduce citrus, onion, avocado, and other migraine trigger foods.
2. Reduce caffeine by ½.
3. Walk 45 minutes a day, 5 days a week.

Results (Record your experiences and results here):

---

1. Less brain fog
2. Feeling more energized from walking
3. Sleepy at first from reducing caffeine, but starting to feel energized.

Nutritional supplements (List any vitamins or

supplements you have identified)

1. Magnesium
2. B2
3. B12 (methylcobalamin form)

Dietary changes (List any specific changes to your diet, e.g. foods to eliminate or to add)

Eliminate or reduce foods that trigger migraine syndrome. Chocolate, red wine, any dark spirits, nuts, citrus, onions, avocado, snap peas, fava beans, fermented foods, yogurt, caffeine.

Super foods (List any super foods you have identified)

Blue green algae.

Herbs and herbal teas (List any herbs and herbal teas you have identified)

Chamomile, passion flower, lavender.

Exercise and movement (List activities such as Qi Gong, Yoga, back strengthening exercises, posture improvements, swimming, stretching and walking)

> Yoga, walking, swimming qi gong. Tapping on back of neck at base of skull.

Practitioners (List providers such as chiropractor, massage therapist, acupuncturist, doctor, and osteopath)

Techniques (list any techniques you have identified, such as Emotional Freedom Technique, energy healing, and Reiki)

> Emotional freedom technique once/day or as needed.

Rituals (List any rituals you have identified)

> 1. Morning meditation.
> 2. Qi gong self-massage and eye relaxation techniques.

Other supports (List supports such as a support group, an informative online community, an accountability partner, a holistic health coach, books, and web sites.)

> Holistic health coach. Book: *Heal Your Headache*, by David Buchholz.

ACKNOWLEDGMENTS

I would like to thank the women who participated in the interviews for this book, whose name and business name follow:

- **Alexandra Roach**: *Holistic Ways - Start Living Healthy & Happy. Today!*
- **Aubree Deimler**: *Wellness Coach at Peace With Endo*
- **Candice Csaky**: *Healthy Wife, Happy Life*
- **Paula M. Youmell**: *Holistic R.N. & Healer*
- **Barbara Searles**: *Bodyworks Integrative Health LLC*
- **Irene Drabkin** – *Certified Holistic Health Counselor, Certified Transformational Coach*

It has been an honor to witness the healing journeys of the women I interviewed, as well as those of many others along the way.

I would like to thank all the members of my Wednesday night metaphysical support group, including Michele Truxillo who leads the group; Carl Rainey, group member and my significant other; Jeri Kagel; Julie Mesmer Wallace; Mary Cobb; Joan White; Kathy Tucker; and Janet Wilson. I also owe a debt to the friends and family who have supported me through writing this book for years. Also, Marina Shevell, my Health Coach and mutual mentoring partner; Elena Oliker, my partner in figuring out how to stay in charge of health; Diane Haavind, friend and first reader, and Melanie Smallie, who initially encouraged me to write a book on how I manage my health 15 years ago.

This book would not have been possible without the tireless support and encouragement of Joshua Rosenthal, founder of the Institute for Integrative Nutrition; Lindsey Smith, author and co-leader of Launch Your Dream Book IIN with Joshua; and the 300+ fellow IIN graduates who formed the supportive community for the birthing of this and many other books on health and wellness. You all rock!

And special thanks to my accountability partner Sara Kleinfeld, my outstanding and amazing editor, Douglas Williams, and my very talented graphic artist, Austin Rubben.

About the Author

When Laura was 26 years old, she first took charge of her own health, after years of dealing with illnesses for which conventional medicine had few answers.

She realized that she was her own best expert, and couldn't stop exploring, researching and pursuing holistic approaches to wellness.

And the rest ... is history.

As a serial entrepreneur and the founder of Intuitive Wellness, she's deeply passionate about inspiring others to learn to take responsibility for their own health and healing.

One client described her as "a wise woman," while another declared her to be "a life saver"!

When she's not working in her organic kitchen garden, you can find her swimming at the Y, practicing Qi Gong and yoga and conducting process improvement projects in corporations.

Meet Laura and stay in-the-know about her upcoming events at www.intuitive-wellness.com.

Laura's Biography

Laura Brown is a Certified Health Coach (CHC) and the Director of Intuitive Wellness, a wellness practice delivering individual, group and community counseling on healthy nutrition and lifestyle. Laura earned her (CHC) designation at the Institute for Integrative Nutrition (IIN), in alliance with Columbia University's Teacher's College. She also is certified by the American Association of Drugless Practitioners (AADP).

Laura serves as an ambassador for the Institute for Integrative Nutrition, contributing to Georgia's communities in particular, as well as the world community at large. She publishes articles on various health topics and speaks regularly at health-oriented events, and for educational and other organizations, on topics such as Brain Health, Longevity and Preventing Chronic Illness Through Diet and Lifestyle.

Laura's background includes more than 20 years in a corporate setting as a business technology consultant, authoring and publishing two books in that arena: Integration Models – Templates for Business Transformation (A SAMS White Book), and Special Edition Using Microsoft CRM (Que). She holds a B.A. in Philosophy from Georgia State University with specific emphasis in Phenomenology and Existentialism.

www.ingramcontent.com/pod-product-compliance
Lightning Source LLC
Chambersburg PA
CBHW072025040426
42447CB00009B/1739